FREE TO LEAD

UNLEASH YOUR HIDDEN LEADERSHIP GENIUS

by
WILL STEEL

STEEL
PUBLICATIONS

Free to Lead: Unleash Your Hidden Leadership Genius
By Will Steel
Published by Steel Publications

AUTHOR'S NOTE: Visit www.willsteel.com/freetolead for more information, tips, resources and strategies designed to help you in your journey to accelerate business growth with authentic leadership and reduce workload stress.

What Others Are Saying...

Will is simply extraordinary. He's the leader's leader, demonstrating a rare and powerful expression of candor, compassion, and unquestionable expertise in his field. When he speaks, lives, businesses and organisations change in the most remarkable of ways. A big time producer in a field where many profess but few deliver.

GARY JOHN BISHOP – NYT Best Selling Author, *Unf*ck Yourself*, garyjohnbishop.com

Free to Lead **isn't simply a book**—it's a transformational journey. Will Steel has crafted an indispensable resource for leaders who are ready to dismantle the barriers of limiting beliefs and harness the power of authentic leadership. With incisive strategies and a clear, actionable path to achieving unstoppable authentic leadership and business growth, this book is essential for anyone eager to elevate their leadership and foster a culture of growth and integrity. If you're ready to unlock your full potential and lead with clarity and unshakeable confidence, this book will show you the way.

CHRISTIAN MICKELSEN – #1 Best Selling author of *Abundance Unleashed,* www.christianmickelsen.com

In twenty years of building businesses and employing over 1,000 people, I've learned that real leadership is about aligning with your team's values, developing others, and letting go of the need for credit or praise.

It's a privilege to endorse Free to Lead, which cuts through outdated leadership models and shows you what it really takes to lead—authentically, powerfully, and with purpose.

Drawing on decades of experience guiding over 90,000 people worldwide, Will Steel challenges you to rethink modern leadership—in a world that needs great leaders more than ever.

ROB MOORE – Entrepreneur, author, and founder of *money.school*

I dedicate this book to my sons, Daniel and Jamie, who grew up without me being there physically most of the time as I led transformational programs all over the planet, yet still love me and appreciate the commitment I have to making a difference in the world. I love you beyond words.

I am also profoundly grateful to my extraordinary clients, whose bravery in confronting and exploring their deepest fears and beliefs enables them to unlock, embrace, and unleash their true greatness. You are all my heroes.

Will

CONTENTS

FOREWORD

I first met Will Steel in the year 2000, at a pivotal moment in my journey of leadership and personal growth. At the time, Will was leading an intensive six-month leadership program in London. His dedication to transformation went beyond geographical boundaries—he saw something in me, a leader capable of bringing change to Egypt. He made sure I didn't just attend the program's weekend workshops in London, he personally guided me through every lesson, discussion, and insight, ensuring I had full access to the experience. His belief in leadership as a way of life, rather than a position or title, shaped my own understanding in ways that continue to impact me to this day.

Since then, I've had the privilege of learning from Will by working alongside him, and most recently, by receiving his guidance as my personal business coach. Over the past year, his coaching has helped me make major breakthroughs—not just in running my company successfully, but in stepping into a greater leadership role, assisting in leadership training, and expanding the concept of innate leadership in the Arab world.

At its core, *Free to Lead* delivers a powerful message: Leadership is not a privilege or a gift; it is a fundamental part of being human. It is not granted by others, nor is it reserved for a select few. Leadership is about choice—the choice to take ownership of your life, to grow emotionally, and to act with intention. It is about deciding to create your own reality rather than waiting for someone else to define it for you.

But making that choice requires a shift in perspective. Many of us hold ourselves back without realising it, believing that external barriers are what keep us from progress. Through my own journey with Will, I came to see that the real obstacles weren't outside of me—they were within me. The moment I let go of those self-imposed limits, my business, my aspirations, and my personal vision all took a massive leap forward.

What makes Will's approach so powerful is his ability to reconnect leadership to fittra—our natural, instinctive state of being. He doesn't teach leadership as a set of techniques or strategies; instead, he guides people back to their own inherent ability to lead. This is the kind of leadership that lasts, that makes an impact, and that continues to grow over time.

The insights in this book are not just theories; they are lived experiences. I have had the honor of assisting Will in his programs and witnessing firsthand how these principles transform lives. His depth of understanding, his wisdom, and his unwavering commitment to human potential make *Free to Lead* an essential guide for anyone ready to take their leadership to the next level.

If you are ready to step into your own leadership—not by following a formula, but by reconnecting with who you truly are—then this book is for you.

Dr. Ahmed Eldemellawy MB BCh, MIBA

Introduction

THE JOURNEY TO AUTHENTIC LEADERSHIP

What is holding you back in your business, in your life, and in your leadership? What's keeping you small, preventing you from chasing your dreams and achieving your goals?

Hint: It's not your circumstances, your past, your intellect, or even your motivation. In fact, the real barrier isn't tangible. It's something that might surprise you—a hidden force that you can uncover and eliminate: limiting beliefs. Now, here's the big problem with limiting beliefs. YOU don't think you have them. You think everyone else has them. You don't have them, but you believe them.

You might think that the experiences you've had shape who you are. But the truth is, it's not what you've gone through that shapes you—it's your interpretation of those events. Throughout this book, I will take you on a journey to show you how your perceptions create limiting beliefs that ultimately dictate who you are and what you do in life—and, more importantly, how to rewrite those narratives, break away from those beliefs, and step into being the *you* that you can be without them. You are phenomenal, and you are capable of anything you put your mind to.

Our perceptions are strong, but they're not immovable. To change our thinking, it takes conscious self-reflection and self-evaluation—but this alone often isn't enough. You also need a framework that gives you access to the source of your limiting beliefs. This book provides that framework, guiding you through a transformational journey, one that first frees you from the inner barriers holding you back, and then empowers you to step into your full potential as a leader and as a human being.

On this journey, I will teach you how to allow old memories to surface, uncover the beliefs that are holding you back, and dismantle those beliefs. Only by doing this inner work can you move forward and step into who you truly are.

Throughout this book, you will learn that when you peel away the layers of your limiting beliefs, automatic reactions, and ingrained behaviours you are able to accomplish so much more than you believe possible. This is the basis of my framework, **The Fittra Method**.

In Chapter 1, I will share more about the origin of this name. It comes from the Arabic word *fittra*, which represents our innate nature, the pure and unaltered state of being that each human being is born with. It is our state before we form our limiting beliefs—before we become influenced by societal conditioning, expectations, or external pressures. It is the true, uncorrupted version of who we are—our authentic selves.

In this book, you will discover your limiting beliefs, automatic reactions, and ingrained behaviours. Then,

you'll learn how to break free from them to uncover your authentic self, enabling you to inspire others, influence those you lead, and impact the world around you.

THE INVISIBLE PRISON OF LIMITING BELIEFS

I've experienced limiting beliefs in many areas of my life. One story springs to mind as an easy example to illustrate how this works.

I spent most of my life refusing to sing. I couldn't sing, and I didn't want anyone to hear me. This was a truth I had accepted, and I never imagined it would change.

But then a composer friend of mine, Simon, came to stay with me for a while. He set up his recording equipment in his bedroom, mixing and bringing music to life. One day, while we were both in the kitchen, I confessed to him, 'I've always wondered if I could sing.'

He told me, 'Well, just sing into the microphone—we'll know straight away.'

I felt a wave of fear wash over me. And all I wanted to do was take back what I had just said.

But I didn't want to admit that I was afraid. 'Sure', I said. 'What should I sing?'

Simon told me he could get the backing track for any song, whatever I wanted.

'Okay. How about "Blowin' in the Wind" by Bob Dylan?'

Simon nodded in agreement. 'Sure, let's do it.'

My heart raced. The thought of singing into the microphone was actually terrifying. I made up an excuse that I was too busy, trying to stall for time and avoid the inevitable excruciating embarrassment I was surely going to experience.

But of course, Simon wasn't going to forget. So I did what anyone would do in my situation—tried to completely avoid him. For the next two weeks, I avoided even walking into the kitchen if I knew he was there. It was like a glass wall between us. I just wanted the entire singing idea to go away.

After a couple of weeks, Simon found me and said, 'Hey Will, I have everything set up for you to sing. Do you wanna come and give it a go?'

Fear gripped me. It felt like the walls were closing in around me.

'Sure,' I said, not wanting to admit my fear.

As I walked up to the microphone, I could feel the fear rising. It felt like I had a concrete collar around my larynx, choking me. I'd have to force my voice through it to make a sound.

I took a deep breath and went for it. And with Simon's help, I finally managed to lay down three takes of the first verse of 'Blowin' in the Wind'.

Afterwards, it felt like I was in limbo. I had no idea if it was good or terrible. Simon is one of those stereotypical cheerful English people—he wouldn't have said anything even if it was awful.

I had an event I needed to head out to, so I left Simon to mix the track.

The next day, when I emerged from my bedroom, Simon was waiting for me with an iPhone in his hand.

'Hey, I've mixed your song. Do you want to hear it?'

'Sure,' I said, hiding my apprehension.

I held my breath as he played it for me, bracing myself for the worst. And I was shocked—it sounded good. I couldn't believe what I was hearing.

'Wow!' I exclaimed. 'Is that really me?'

Simon responded, 'Yup, sounds pretty good' (aka *very good* in English expression). 'You can sing just as good as anyone out there. You just need to train your voice, that's all.'

I was blown away. I thought to myself, *'If only I'd known I could sing, I'd have been a rock star.'*

But why was this such an earth-shattering moment for me? Why was singing this frightening barrier? Why was I so convinced that I was a terrible singer—when I'd never even tried? I had to dig deep to discover the answer to those questions. Using the technique Identifying Your Stories, which I will unpack in Chapter 4 (a part of The Fittra Method), I searched for the moment that created this limiting belief...

THE MOMENT MY LIMITING BELIEF WAS FORMED

It all centered around an event that happened when I was eight years old. My class was rehearsing for the school concert, singing our little heads off, when Ms. Bland, our teacher, shushed us. 'Okay, the first two rows, you can be quiet for a moment. I just want to hear Christopher.' Christopher was standing right behind me in the third row.

My stomach sank. I thought that I'd been silenced because my singing wasn't good. And right there, I decided, *'I must sound awful.'*

And that was the glass ceiling I placed on myself, one I carried all the way into adulthood. I refused to sing in front of anyone for 40 years, terrified to even try. I was convinced that if I did, it would sound awful.

This is just a simple revelation—not one that changed the course of my life. (I didn't become a rock star, although I have since written and recorded my own songs.) The point is that I held myself back in this area due to fear that originated from a decision I'd made in my past at eight years old.

You might be thinking of your own example, something you've been too afraid to do or try, something you've believed about yourself your whole life.

We're all carrying these kinds of limiting beliefs around, constraints we've placed on ourselves due to our perceptions of events in the past. Those perceptions become our reality. But we can learn to break away from them and let ourselves be so much more than we currently allow ourselves to be. Consider that there are no real limits in reality—they're all unconsciously self-imposed.

HOW TO READ THIS BOOK: A TWO-PART JOURNEY

As I said previously, this book is designed to guide you through a transformative journey. In order to fully step into authentic leadership, you must first dismantle the limiting beliefs and internal constraints that have shaped your experience up until now. Only by doing this inner work can you create the foundation needed to lead with clarity, confidence, and authenticity.

Part 1: Shattering Your Limiting Beliefs

This book is divided into two main parts. The first part is intended to enable you to identify and transform your limiting beliefs. As you work your way through each chapter, you will see the different ways limiting beliefs have impacted you. You could think of each chapter as a facet of a diamond—each one gives you a unique perspective of what has been going on in your life, and is a gateway to the source of your limiting beliefs. Once you find the source of a limiting belief, you can own it, be responsible for it, and move beyond it. As you move through the chapters of this book, each one will uncover a different limiting belief. And with each revelation, you'll begin to reclaim a part of yourself that has long been diminished—some more deeply than others. So don't be concerned if certain chapters resonate more strongly than others. They're all working together to ultimately set the real *you* free.

As we walk through this book together, we'll explore the various constraints that limit your freedom. Along the way, I'll share stories from my own journey, as well as examples from clients (with names changed to protect their confidentiality) to help bring these ideas to life. I will also be asking you to do exercises to help you break away from the limiting beliefs you are carrying. In this way, you will be able to dismantle the box you have been living inside of.

(I recommend that you work through these exercises in a designated notebook that you set aside for this work. This will allow you to keep everything in one place and revisit the work whenever you need to.)

Part 2: Creating Your Authentic Leadership

Once you have shattered your limiting beliefs in order to clear space, you'll be opened up and empowered to step into your authentic leadership. In Part 2, we will build on the work you've done in Part 1 to support you in authentically creating your leadership with integrity and purpose. You will learn strategies for becoming a leader, who not only excels in business, but also inspires, influences, and empowers others to be true to themselves.

After this second part, you will no longer grapple with the stress and anxiety that comes when you are working against your true nature. This is where you step into the role of the leader you were always meant to be, the leader you were born to be.

My greatest hope for you, the reader, is that you fully immerse yourself in this book and transform who you are for yourself and others. I have spent the last 27 years leading transformative programs and coaching people to get what is blocking them unblocked and out of their way, opening them up to who they really are, and what they are truly capable of. Once you get everything out of your way you will discover your leadership genius.

If you're tired of playing small, accepting less, and going through life the way you just happened to end up—all while knowing in your heart of hearts that you were meant for so much more—this book is for you.

Most entrepreneurs and business leaders think they just need more information. They read book after book, take course after course, waiting for something to finally click and make everything change. But in my experience, it's not about more information. It's about doing the inner work that breaks you out of your patterns and frees you to move forward and take the steps to live as the real you.

And when you do that, not only will you reconnect with your true self, you'll begin to produce results you never dreamed were possible.

Ultimately, the goal of this book is to set the real *you* free—free to live and free to lead, so you can be a force of nature as you realise your vision in the world.

As you work through the exercises in this book, you also have access to a free video of me working with clients to uncover and dismantle their limiting beliefs. You'll see exactly how the process unfolds and how you can apply it in your own life. You can download it at www.willsteel.com/freetolead.

—Will Steel

PART 1

Shattering Your Limiting Beliefs

Chapter 1

THE FITTRA METHOD: FREEING YOUR TRUE SELF

'The journey of becoming an authentic leader is essentially a journey back to fittra.'

Two years after I started my coaching business, one of my dear clients, Dr. Ahmed Eldemellawy, who runs a very successful health business throughout the Middle East, said to me, 'What we really need in the Middle East is a leadership program, particularly for women.'

I said, 'Okay, let's create one.' So, we set to work. We met every week for a year to flesh out ideas, focusing on ways to free people up to become the natural leader we all have within us.

When we submitted our application to register our business in Dubai, we had to come up with three possible names. Dr. Ahmed suggested "Fittra Leadership Institute".

I wasn't familiar with the term at the time, but once he explained it to me, I knew it was the perfect name for our programs in the Middle East.

The word fittra does not have a direct translation into English, it is seen as the primordial state of purity and innocence in which all humans are created. It represents an inherent recognition of truth, goodness, and the divine. In this context, fittra also symbolises a natural inclination towards compassion, integrity, and a connection with the Creator. But beyond religious or philosophical understanding, fittra embodies something universal and profoundly relevant to everyone, regardless of their background. **It is the idea that each of us has a core self that is fundamentally aligned with truth and goodness. It's who we really are.**

Fittra captured what we were committed to accomplishing. Rather than people leading the way they thought they were supposed to lead, or being constrained by limiting beliefs, we wanted to give people access to leading as their authentic selves—living their fittra, unconstrained and limitless.

The journey of becoming an authentic leader is essentially a journey back to fittra. It is about stripping away the layers of conditioning, limiting beliefs, and fears that we picked up throughout our lives. These layers often act as barriers to the expression of our true selves, leading us to act in ways that are disconnected from our deeper values and purpose. **Authentic leadership, therefore, is about leading from that place of natural alignment—leading from our fittra.**

True leadership does not come from adopting external personas or trying to fit into predefined moulds. Instead, it comes from being deeply connected to who we are at our core and leading from that place of truth. When you lead from fittra, you lead with integrity, clarity, and courage.

In the context of this book, embracing your fittra means aligning your leadership, business, and life with your true nature. By doing so, you not only free yourself to lead authentically but also create an environment where others feel empowered to express their true selves, which creates a ripple effect that can transform not only your business but also the lives of those around you.

These are the core philosophies and goals behind The Fittra Method that you will learn in this book. Applying this method will free you not only from limiting beliefs but also the automatic behaviours and reactions that have shaped and constrained your life up to now.

Case Study: Martin's Transformation in Leadership and Marriage

Martin was a successful real estate broker facing a dual crisis: a struggling business and a marriage on the verge of collapse—a situation that, sadly, isn't uncommon among entrepreneurs. He loved his wife but felt deeply disconnected from her. In his case, the distance between them was rooted in a secret he'd never shared: He had cheated on her before they were married. This unspoken truth weighed heavily on him, causing significant stress and a lack of authenticity in both his personal and professional life. Over time, he had formed a view of himself that he was a terrible person.

Through my coaching, Martin was encouraged to confront his fear and reveal the truth to his wife. It was a daunting step—but at that point, with his situation at its lowest and nothing left to lose, it was also the only way forward. It was necessary for true transformation.

When Martin finally confessed, he was met with understanding and forgiveness, which reignited their relationship. More importantly, he was able to create a new narrative for himself, one of being honest and transparent. This honesty spilled over into his professional life, where he began leading with greater transparency and authenticity, aligning with his true fittra.

Martin's experience underscores the power of honesty and vulnerability in leadership. By addressing personal issues, embracing authenticity, and separating out what happened from all the stories he had been telling himself over the years, he not only saved his marriage but also revitalised his business, creating a more cohesive and motivated team.

Case Study: André's Discovery of His Limiting Belief

André was a coach who helped founders build the skills they needed to create successful, thriving businesses. His work was powerful, paving the way for his clients to skyrocket their businesses. And yet, despite the value he brought to the table, he was charging well below what he should have been charging. Logically, André *knew* this. But he couldn't seem to bring himself to raise his rates up to the industry standard.

Through The Fittra Method, André discovered the source of his inability to ask for what his coaching was really worth. When he was a child, while attempting to follow some older boys, he had fallen off his bike, experiencing a painful injury. However, in that moment, it was not the injury that hurt him the most. What hurt him was the words he told himself—that he couldn't do what the other boys could, that he was 'less than'. He carried this underlying belief throughout his life.

In his coaching business, he couldn't raise his rates because, deep down, he believed that what he did wasn't as good as what 'others' could do and that he couldn't ask for what 'others' were charging.

This belief kept André not only from seeing his own value and charging accordingly but also from showing up fully in his life and his business, with confidence, as the leader he truly was. We were able to rewrite the narrative that he had been carrying for so long, reframing the fall off the bicycle from being a sign of being less than to being a demonstration of how courageous he was. He overcame his limiting belief and was able to change his entire perspective on his coaching services. Before implementing The Fittra Method, he was bringing in $125,000 a year. Within just five weeks, he was on track to more than *double that* to $320,000. The Fittra Method helped André recognise the limits that had been holding him back and helped him rewrite the story he'd been telling himself. From that point on, he stepped into his authentic, limitless self—able to powerfully and freely ask for what his coaching was truly worth, which was more than double what he'd been charging. He's now, at the time of writing, on track for his first million-dollar year.

Case Study: Dan's Breakthrough with Money and Self-Worth

Dan, a talented and brilliant scientist, had developed a successful method for helping people lose weight safely and sustainably. But despite his expertise, like André, he was charging clients a fee far below the industry standard, leading to burnout and financial strain. Through coaching and applying The Fittra Method, Dan uncovered a deep-seated discomfort with money stemming from past experiences of being manipulated.

The root of Dan's issues was traced back to a traumatic childhood incident with his godfather. Because of this incident, he believed that people would try to own him and manipulate him. Deep down, he believed something was wrong with him. He went through life wary of financial transactions and success. If he started to get any rewards for his accomplishments, such as a bonus or recognition, he would feel uncomfortable and leave the organisation he was working for. He wasn't going to let people believe they could own him.

A breakthrough came when Dan recognised how the decisions he'd made about himself, others, and life around this past trauma had been unconsciously influencing his business practices. By addressing these emotional blocks, Dan was able to break away from his limiting beliefs, create a new narrative, raise his fees significantly so that they aligned with the value he provided, and delegate much of his work to trained associates.

This change allowed Dan to work less while earning more, creating a healthier balance in his life. His story highlights the importance of understanding and transforming deep-seated hidden beliefs that limit our potential, particularly those related to self-worth and money.

Whether you realise it or not, just like the clients above, you are being held back by stories from your past. If you practise what is in this book, you can untangle the web of

constraints you've placed on yourself and embrace your full potential to live and lead powerfully, fully, and freely—in fittra.

Chapter 2

THE JOURNEY FROM FEAR TO FITTRA

'You have all the answers; you've just not been asked the right questions.'

In early 2020, I was let go from my job, something that is an almost universally scary event. But the truth was I didn't feel fear. I knew that the universe was opening up a door for me—one I had been scared to open up myself, but one that I was ready to walk through.

By this time in my life, I was already on the journey to conquering my limiting beliefs and moving forward into my true, authentic self. So what I felt wasn't fear but validation and excitement about the chance to be the master of my own destiny.

However, when I think about moments in my life when I *did* feel fear—the kind that holds you back from stepping into new opportunities—one stands out pretty solidly.

I spent 12 years as a pilot. It was a career that I enjoyed

and one that I worked hard at. But at that time, I hadn't experienced the transformation you're going through in this book. I was still holding onto limiting beliefs that were so strong they kept me in patterns of fear and self-sabotage.

After ten years in the Royal Air Force, where I received world-renowned training and three trophies— one for leadership, one for aerobatics, and one for fast jet low-level navigation, I transitioned to a commercial airline role with a British Airways franchise. A year later, I applied for another position, this time directly with British Airways rather than a franchise. The interview process went very well. I was even told that I had achieved some of the highest pilot aptitude scores British Airways had seen in years. They offered me the opportunity to fly Boeing 747-400s on long-haul flights out of London Heathrow. This was a dream job for most pilots, a top position that any pilot would be proud to take.

But I hesitated. I told myself that in such a prestigious position, I wouldn't get enough hands-on experience flying the aircraft—much of it would be on autopilot. I couldn't shake off the fear that without constant practice, I would fail the manual flying part of my annual instrument rating. This fear of failure, this belief that I wasn't actually that good, sent me spiraling into the worst-case scenario. I imagined failing an assessment, losing my job, destroying my career—and the biggest fear was everyone finding out that I wasn't as good as they thought I was.

I declined the offer. My pilot friends were shocked. They couldn't believe I would turn down this opportunity. And on paper, I had no reason to. I was qualified. I had the scores. I had the experience. I was ready. But none of that mattered.

My self-doubt ran too deep. I couldn't overcome the limiting belief that I wasn't good enough and would ultimately fail.

Just a couple of years later, I left the aviation industry altogether, largely because of that decision. It haunted me. And it wasn't until years later that I truly understood why I panicked and how deeply my limiting beliefs ran.

When I look back at these two moments, I can't help but compare them. A prestigious opportunity that I ran away from, led by fear, and a moment where I lost my job but felt only confidence and excitement. You would think that my responses would have been the opposite. But I wasn't the same person in the first scenario as I was in the second, just as you won't be the same person you are now by the time you have completed this book.

(Imagine, for a moment, what that might look like for you. What fears are you holding onto that will be overcome? What doubts do you have that will be shattered? And what will you be able to reach for when you release the anchors holding you back?)

In 2020, at the time I was let go, I was already well-practised in the work of uncovering limited beliefs. I had discovered many over the years that I'd been unaware of. I no longer lived in the box I had originally ended up in. I was ready to let the *real* me step forward.

Standing in my kitchen after being told I was let go, I vowed to myself, *'Never again will I work for an organisation. I will be the master of my own destiny.'*

I started coaching—at first because it was something I knew I could do immediately until I worked out what I really wanted to do—but it soon became a passion.

There is nothing more fulfilling to me than seeing someone break through their constraints and produce results way beyond what they ever imagined. I want this for *you* and for everyone who is up for the game of expanding the impact that they can have in the world. In fact, that's what drove me to write this book—the desire to give as many people as possible access to my framework, The Fittra Method.

WHO THIS BOOK IS FOR

This book is for you if you know deep down that you are not being as effective as you would like to be as a leader. Whether you are the leader of a large corporation, a serial entrepreneur, a business owner, or in any leadership role in an organisation, or even if you don't feel you are providing leadership in your family, friend circles, or community. What you will discover is that you have invisible constraints holding back the real YOU and what you have to say.

I believe, after working with over 90,000 people all over the world, that we are all capable of leadership —not just those with titles such as leader, manager, boss, or owner.

To be a leader is to be someone who speaks up, someone who speaks their truth—not to prove they are right or that others are wrong, but to impact what is going on in the moment. A leader calls it the way that it is, not the way they'd like it to be or want others to think that it is. In short they are free to speak up, free to make a difference, and free to lead.

If you don't currently feel you are that kind of leader 100% of the time, or you have to rely on getting loud, angry, or even forceful to produce the results you want, this book is for you.

The Fittra Method is intended to have you strip away all the facade and get you back to who you really are. You are a force of nature—the real you has no limits. All the limits you have are self-imposed. You have all the answers; you've just not been asked the right questions. If you start with this premise and follow the framework in this book (The Fittra Method), you are in for a profound shift in who you *know yourself* to be.

You might think you are here to learn how to be a stronger leader. The truth is that you are here to discover the leader that you really are, the one who has been hidden below the surface, behind layers of limiting beliefs and misidentifications that you have related to as you.

My goal is to help you uncover the barriers you've unwittingly built, so you can move past the diminished, fearful version of yourself and become the bold, powerful, authentic leader you were always meant to be.

SELF-ASSESSMENT: FREEDOM AND POWER CHECK-IN EXERCISE

Before we proceed with the rest of the book, let's first check in with where you're at right now in both business and life. Below, rate how accurate each statement is for you on a scale of 1 – 5 with 1 being 'not accurate at all' and 5 being 'most accurate'.

Then, total up your scores and use the Answer Key to determine your next steps.

FREEDOM AND POWER CHECK-IN: SELF-RATING STATEMENTS

1. I have full power when dealing with breakdowns and failures in my business.	
2. I enjoy working with my current clients and customers.	
3. I have more than enough clients and customers for my needs.	
4. I consistently hit my revenue goals on time and on target.	
5. I feel at peace in my business and rarely spend time thinking about my business outside of set business hours.	
6. I can take 3 - 4 weeks of vacation per year completely unplugged from my business without interruption, and my company continues to grow without me.	
7. I can fully express myself with every single person in my company.	
8. When I walk into my business, I feel totally at home.	
9. I love all the people I work with.	
10. I feel confident that the team I work with has totally got my back and I trust them 100%.	
11. I have full support from the people in my life outside of work.	
12. I have total confidence and power in the following areas:	
Work	
Family	

All my relationships	
All my friendships	
With everyone in my community	
Finances	
Health	
Sport and leisure	

TOTAL UP YOUR SCORE:

Answer Key for What Your Score Really Means

Score: 20 – 40

You feel limited and are likely lacking authenticity in most, if not all, aspects of your business and life. The bad news is that stress and anxiety are taking a heavy toll. The good news? By confronting the truth about your situation, you have an incredible opportunity to strip away false beliefs and rediscover your authentic self. The Fittra Method offers a transformative path to redesign your life and business from the ground up. Study this book with an open mind, do all the exercises, and you will have a huge shift in confidence and how you experience yourself in all aspects of your life.

Score: 41 – 75

You are probably comfortable, making a decent living, but feel that something is missing. You might tell yourself you just need to work harder or be disciplined. Most people settle and stay here, living their lives just going through the motions. I don't want that for you. You could easily have so much more. With this book and the exercises within it, you can radically alter your life and experience being fully alive.

Score: 76+

You're 'successful' on the surface, but deep down, you know you were meant for more. For you, the real challenge is to read this book like you've never heard any of this kind of information before. And the potential pitfall to watch out for is to read this book thinking, 'I know this already.' What you 'know' can get in the way of you discovering your true self. You can discover a new *you* beyond anything you can imagine right now. You may have even heard that kind of phrase before. I encourage you to stay curious and open-minded, to let go of what you've tried in the past, and dive in fully, committing to doing the exercises and the work asked of you as you go through this book.

Chapter 3

Gaining Clarity About What You Want

'You are bound by invisible constraints; some of which you are aware of and many more that you are not.'

I'm going to say something that might be hard to hear, but it's something I wish I'd heard earlier in my life. You live in a small, constrained box. You've told yourself things that have kept you small. 'I can't do this,' 'I'm not good at that,' 'I'm not X enough,' 'I'm not Y,' 'They think this, but I'm really that...' and on and on. You have created glass ceilings for yourself and put walls around who you really are. You are like a trained flea.

You might bristle at that analogy, but stick with me for a moment. The way you train fleas is very simple. You put some untrained fleas in a box or jar and simply place a glass lid on the container. Fleas can naturally jump way higher than the height of the container, so at first, they bang their heads against the lid, which must be pretty painful. But fleas are also actually quite intelligent. They soon work out that if they only jump a certain height, they won't get hurt. And after a while, you can remove the lid. The fleas won't jump out to freedom; they are now trained. They believe they will get hurt if they jump any higher than where the lid was, so they remain trapped in the confines of a prison, even with no actual lid constraining them. They are trapped inside their perception of what is and isn't possible.

Similar to fleas, you have trained yourself not to jump too high. You have put glass ceilings on your self-expression, your goals and desires, your freedom to speak up and say what needs to be said, and your ability to accomplish what you really are capable of accomplishing. Because of this, you have limited yourself and who you really are. Consider that you are bound by invisible constraints, some of which you are aware of and many more that you are not.

HOW WE CREATE OUR OWN GLASS BOX

If there's one thing I feel certain about after coaching so many leaders through their transformations, it's that the universe will help you if you tell the truth about what you really want. The problem is we have become so conditioned in our thinking and in our belief systems that we're no longer in touch with what we want.

When you were a kid, and you saw an athlete or someone you admired, like a rock star or a doctor, you said, 'I want to do that!' But let's say you wanted to be a doctor; then you found out that doctors need to be good at chemistry and biology—and you don't do well in those subjects. Without realising it, you closed a door for yourself. Now, being a doctor is out of the question for you. Or perhaps someone insulted you or called you ugly—now you've decided you're unattractive. So, you never put yourself out there to pursue the romantic relationships you truly desire. Again and again, as you go through life, more and more doors close. You don't just have a glass ceiling; you've enclosed yourself in a multifaceted glass box. You no longer dream and imagine what's possible for you. Instead, you're resigned to who you are in life, and you go through it settling for mediocrity.

If we want to shatter the glass box we've created for ourselves, we first need to discover that our limitations aren't actually real. We created them somewhere in the past, in some moment of stress or upset. It *is* possible to get back to those moments, even the ones you've forgotten, to reexamine the decisions you made that now limit you. Once you see that it is *you* who decided that you weren't good enough, or that the world isn't safe, or that something bad will happen if you do XYZ, the constraints will fall away. You'll find yourself no longer limited by those past decisions, which became your limiting beliefs. What once seemed impossible will now appear as possible—and the experience will be one of amazement and excitement—like 'Wow!'

UNDERSTANDING OUR GOALS AND DESIRES

In Chapter 1, I shared the story of losing my job but feeling excited about the door that was opening up for me. For the first time, I felt free to create the life I really wanted, living on my own terms. Many people in that situation might not have felt that way, but this excitement was a result of the work

I was doing on myself. I was using the tools that we will be exploring in this book. I knew that I could have anything I really wanted—even if I didn't know what it was in that moment. In fact, I had just worked through a powerful tool called "The Deathbed Exercise" (which you will work through for yourself at the end of this chapter).

It changed my entire perspective. Nothing about my job was leading me to the path that I really wanted. But I had been living in fear. I had been staying in the jar, afraid to go out on my own. I'd been conditioned to believe that it was better to stay comfortable and have a regular, meager salary than to take the risk of quitting that job and creating my own business.

The Deathbed Exercise opened my eyes. I discovered that my regret on my deathbed would be that I had never had the courage to leave my job. Two days later, I was let go. Talk about the universe intervening! It was as if it was saying, 'Okay, you don't have the courage to leave? Well, here you go.' Boom.

Just the realisation that I had been living a lie contextualised what was happening. Ordinarily, losing your job would be a fearful experience, but for me, given that I'd just done this exercise, it was freeing. I knew that what was happening was exactly what needed to happen.

Now, given you are reading this book, consider you are in the right place at the right time; there are no accidents. You have the opportunity right now to start telling the truth about what's not working in your life. What are you putting up with? What are you tolerating or settling for? What are you accepting without checking in with yourself to see if it's what you really want? Do you really love where you are right now? Do you really love what you're doing in life right now? By challenging yourself and telling the truth about what you don't love, you open up the opportunity to have this book help you get what you really want.

THE DEATHBED EXERCISE

First, set yourself up in a quiet room where you won't be disturbed. A bedroom is ideal. Place your designated notebook and a pen or pencil next to your bed and open to a blank page. Then follow these steps:

1. Close the curtains and switch off the light. Lie down on the bed and close your eyes. Take a few deep, slow breaths.

2. Imagine you are really old. It is the final day of your life, and there you are, lying down, waiting to die. Picture your loved ones gathered around your bed. You are fully awake, but you don't want to open your eyes and have to look at their sad faces of concern. You hear the doctor telling someone outside, 'They only have a few hours left—they're really close to the end now.'

3. Imagine this is really it. It's the end of your life, and time has run out. There is no tomorrow. There is no later.

4. Now look into yourself. Tune in to what you're feeling and see if you can find any feelings of regret. However slight they may be, follow them. Ask yourself, 'What is it that I regret?' (What have you done that you wish you hadn't done? What have you not accomplished that you wished you had? What have you never even attempted

that you regret not trying? What opportunities did you not take advantage of?)

5. Stay with this feeling until an answer arises. (This can hit you like a bolt of lightning.)

6. If an answer doesn't come, simply say, 'What I regret is ___' and finish the sentence.

7. Once you've seen something, don't just settle for that, repeat the process. Look for any other feelings of regret, get in touch with any that show up. Don't rush. Let yourself feel any regrets that might be there. Keep asking yourself, 'What else do I regret?'

8. Continue to do this until there really are no more feelings of regret.

9. When you are satisfied, you are done; open your eyes. As soon as you do, grab the pad of paper and note down the regrets you realised.

Next, answer the following questions:

What is it that I really do want to be doing with my life?
What do I really want?
What truly matters to me?
What kind of leader do I want to be?
What impact do I want to make in the world?
Write down your answers. They will be useful as you work through the rest of this book.

CHAPTER TAKEAWAYS:

» We often lie to ourselves about what we truly want, consequently chasing things that don't align with our values and purpose. This ultimately creates a sense of unfulfillment.

» Gaining true clarity on what we want—and what we don't want—gives us direction in life.

» What often gets in the way of being connected to what we really want is telling ourselves that we're okay with what we already have.

Chapter 4

THE STORIES WE TELL OURSELVES

'The stories we tell ourselves aren't based on facts.'

The stories we tell ourselves aren't based on facts—they're shaped by the way we interpreted our experiences. Every interaction and decision is filtered through a personal lens we've developed over time. This forms a private narrative that shapes who we think we are. When we can identify the key moments that formed that lens—and begin to re-examine and reinterpret them—we can break free from the limiting beliefs that have been running the show.

PERSONAL NARRATIVE AND IDENTITY

When I was three years old, my entire family gathered for a special occasion. As everyone sat around, sharing memories, my father started telling the story of how I came into the world. While looking at me, he told everyone, 'We couldn't afford to have a third baby, then Mum got pregnant. We already had two boys, so we were looking forward to having a little girl, and then YOU popped out; you should have been a little girl!'

Everyone burst out laughing—even my grandmothers. But my heart sank. For me, this was devastating: the worst news I had ever heard. What I made that mean to myself was that they didn't want me in the first place—and, what they *really* wanted was a girl. In a defiant declaration to compensate for not being wanted, I determined right there and then that 'I'm the best.'

THE IMPACT OF EARLY INTERPRETATIONS

From that moment on, I felt that I had to prove myself. The decision I made as a three-year-old shaped the course of my entire life. I decided, 'I'm the best!' And I spent my whole life striving to make that true, even in things I wasn't interested in. I won every single race and event at my junior school, filling a drawer with first-place ribbons.

But no matter how many achievements I racked up, it was never enough. I was always chasing the next big thing, telling myself that if I could accomplish *that*, that would be it—I would be the best.

This relentless drive came with significant costs. I often felt isolated because I couldn't let anyone see my vulnerability or insecurity. The fear of not being good enough meant I pushed myself to the brink, sacrificing my relationships and personal well-being. The pressure was immense, and despite my outward success, I lived in a constant state of striving. No matter what I accomplished, it was never enough, leading me to search for the next mountain to climb. And the mountains

I chose got bigger and more challenging as I went through life.

RE-EXPERIENCING YOUR EXPERIENCE

You might be thinking of a similar story from your childhood—something you overheard or experienced, something that stuck with you. Don't shy away from this. The more you can get yourself back there to re-experience the experience, the more you can heal yourself. Imagine and let yourself feel what it actually felt like for you in that moment. What were the feelings and emotions you felt? Imagine you are transported back in time to that moment, like it is actually happening now. Then, once you are there, look and see what you made it mean about *you*, *others*, or *life*. From there, try to get in touch with how your interpretation of the event (not the event itself) has shaped you and your life. How have the decisions you made held you back or left you feeling a need to prove yourself or compensate in some way? How have the stories changed what you reach for or how you show up in the world?

Dwelling in the experience and emotional weight of these early interpretations and decisions is crucial —even when, or especially when, it feels uncomfortable.

For me, this meant revisiting that moment of origin and similar moments to get in touch with both how I felt in those moments, and what I said to myself. And, it's important to not rush through this. I dwell in the experience until I actually feel and experience being there. Then I look to see what I said to myself, what was my understanding and interpretation in that moment. Once I've seen and experienced this newly, I can then look at how my decisions have shaped my behaviour and influenced the way I've experienced life.

In my case, that's when I realised I had wasted my life making up for a decision that had been made by an upset three-year-old. What I had *made it mean* was not the same as what had actually happened. I was dumbfounded and relieved all at the same time.

THE POWER OF INTERPRETATION

It took me a long time to understand why I was so driven and so competitive. I couldn't just do something for enjoyment—I *had* to win. I had to be the best. It wasn't until I was an adult, attending a self-help program, that I had a breakthrough.

Finally, after so many years, I saw the significance I'd given to my father's words and the impact that my assigned meaning had had on my entire life. I also discovered that there was a difference between what happened and what I made it mean. I realised that my parents' words were not about me personally. They hadn't even met me yet when they expressed a preference for a girl. If I were in their shoes, I might have wanted a girl, too, just for a change.

It didn't mean I was unwanted or unloved. It didn't even have anything to do with me. This realisation was life-altering. A lifetime of suppressed emotions welled up inside me, and I sobbed for about ten minutes straight. But when the shock passed, I felt a profound sense of freedom. For the first time, the weight of needing to prove myself to be the best was lifted off of my shoulders. I could just be myself. There was nowhere to get to—I felt whole and complete and at peace with myself and life.

Afterwards, when I shared my discovery with my parents, they were in disbelief. My mother exclaimed, 'What are you talking about? You were the favourite. We picked you up and spoiled you more than the others. You were our little baby.'

This was something that resonated with me. But as a child, I couldn't experience my mother's love. The limiting belief I carried kept me from experiencing anyone's love—not just in my family but later in romantic relationships as well. I found myself suspicious of women, believing they must want something *from* me, not just me.

UNDERSTANDING LIMITING BELIEFS

As you read through this book, you're going to access your own realisations, and that may bring up some emotions. Don't be concerned. It's all part of this fascinating journey of self-discovery. Doing this work is life-altering. It's wonderful. As you release yourself from these limitations, you will start to grow as a human being. Allow the book to work on you – especially when you're away from it.

You might wake up in the middle of the night with a sudden insight about a forgotten incident from your past—a moment when you made a life-shaping decision. This is not unusual when you engage in this kind of inquiry. In fact, it's fascinating. You will learn to love this way of looking at your life.

As you see and understand these moments and separate the story you told yourself from the events themselves, you will open up access to the real you—the unlimited you, in fittra.

The ability to separate events from your interpretation will open up your life and change the way you see your past, your present, and your perceived future.

Your interpretations from the past are strong. They feel real, and they have shaped who you have become in life.

We've all had thoughts, accepted them as true, and they then became beliefs—limiting beliefs. As you have gone through life, you have subconsciously gathered evidence for these beliefs. Over time, they don't live as beliefs; they live as the truth for you. And that's what needs to be altered.

However, identifying our beliefs can be difficult. After all, they don't always jump out—like 'I feel unworthy' or 'I don't believe I'm good enough.' They're often much more subtle and harder to uncover.

You might have found yourself saying phrases like 'It's just the way it is' 'It's just the way I am.' Don't be fooled. These are your limiting beliefs surfacing. They were likely born in moments of high emotional intensity from your past—often during childhood—and they became reinforced over time. The following exercise can help you get to the root of your beliefs and start to reframe them.

EXERCISE: UNCOVERING THE BELIEFS BEHIND YOUR SELF-TALK

To begin transforming these limiting beliefs, you need to identify the repeated familiar phrases you say to yourself— things like 'I'm not that good at X' or 'They don't like me' or 'I'm not that type of a person' or 'There I go again, screwing it up—typical' or 'I'm so stupid.' As you start to identify these phrases, for example, 'I'm so stupid,' ask yourself, 'Where did

"I'm so stupid" start in my life?' What's the earliest time you can remember thinking to yourself, 'I'm so stupid'? Maybe you couldn't figure something out, or maybe someone told you, 'You're stupid.' This is just an example of how to force yourself to get back to remembering the moments you first had these thoughts and decided they were true (aka where you formed these limiting beliefs). Sometimes, these moments are easy to trace back. But often, they require a bit more digging. This exercise can help you start to uncover your limiting beliefs.

To begin, turn to a blank page in your notebook and divide it into three columns.

In the first column, write down significant events from your past that you can remember. In the second column, write the interpretations, meanings you created, or decisions you made from those events. In the third column, write how these interpretations have shaped you and your life.

For example:

Event	Interpretation / Meaning I gave	How It Shaped Me
Parents told me they had wanted a girl	I'm not wanted; I have to prove that I'm the best!	Constantly striving to prove that I'm the best but never feeling satisfied
Teacher told us to shush	I sound awful; no one can ever hear me sing	Terrified to sing if I thought anyone could hear, feeling embarrassed

Dwelling in the Emotional Weight

Before creating a new narrative, it's important to dwell in and connect with the emotional weight these interpretations have had on your life. This makes the exercise more real and gives whatever you create more power.

Start with getting yourself back to the moment you remember. What was it like for you to hear what you heard, to see what you saw, smell what you smelled, and think what you thought? See if you can actually get yourself back there, feeling what you felt in that moment. Don't rush this. Let yourself fully experience the feelings. This is part of the healing process.

Next, look at how your interpretation of the experience **influenced the way you felt, behaved, and related to life—** both in that moment and over time. How did constantly striving for approval affect your relationships, your career, or your well-being? How did the fear of failure shape the choices you made or the opportunities you avoided?

For instance, in my case, the belief *'I'm not wanted; I have to prove that I'm the best'* showed up in many ways:

- I constantly pushed myself to achieve more.
- I found it difficult to form deep, meaningful relationships because I was driven to be the best rather than just enjoying the other person.
- I was never at peace, or satisfied with my achievements, always chasing the next challenge to prove myself.

Reframing Your Narrative

Once you've fully acknowledged the **emotional weight** and the **effect** of your interpretations, the next step is to reframe them. Look at each interpretation and ask yourself if it's truly serving you. If it is not, create a new, empowering narrative.

For example:

Event	Old Interpretation	New Narrative
Parents told me they had wanted a girl	I'm not wanted; I have to prove that I'm the best!	My parents' desire was not about me; I am perfect the way I am
Teacher told us to shush	I sound awful. No one can ever hear me sing	I can learn to do anything I want, I have a great, unique voice

The Power of New Narratives

Reframing your narrative can create profound shifts in your life. By changing the way you interpret past events, you begin to alter your beliefs—and with that, your behaviour. This shift can lead to greater confidence, clearer decision-making, and a deeper sense of freedom and authenticity.

If you only did this one thing—identifying the early incidents where you made limiting decisions, fully feeling the weight of living inside them, and then reframing your narrative—you would already be well on your way to becoming your true self, in fittra.

This foundational step is one of the most powerful ways to transform your life. And as the rest of the chapters unfold, you'll discover more concepts, exercises, and practices to deepen your experience of being your true self.

ONGOING PRACTISE: DISMANTLING LIMITING BELIEFS

Set aside time each week to revisit and reframe one story from your past. Use the following steps:

1. Start by identifying where you are currently feeling weak, constrained, unable to express yourself, fearful, or unable to impact what is happening in a particular situation you are dealing with.
2. Get in touch with how this actually makes you feel and then ask yourself, 'What memory does this remind me of ?'
3. Identify the earliest event from your past when you can remember feeling this way. Ask yourself, 'What actually happened?'
4. Take the time to get yourself back to the moment and reexperience what you felt in that moment.
5. Ask yourself, 'What did I decide when this happened?' (This is your old interpretation)
6. Reflect on and write out how this interpretation has influenced your beliefs, your behaviour, the way you've related to others, your relationships, and your sense of self.
7. Challenge the validity of the old interpretation.
8. Create a new, empowering narrative.
9. Write down the new narrative and repeat it to yourself daily.
10. For even greater power, share what you uncovered—the event, what you made it mean, the decision you made, and how that decision has shaped your life—with the people who are important to you. This will free you even more, and deepen and expand the results of doing this work.

Remember, the stories you tell yourself are just that— stories. You have the power to rewrite them and create a new narrative that supports your growth and success.

REFLECTION QUESTIONS

1. What are some recurring phrases I find myself saying? (E.g. 'I'm so stupid.' 'I always screw it up.')
2. When was the first time I thought that or felt that way?
3. What was actually happening at that moment?
4. Was that an accurate, fair assessment of the situation, or was it a limiting belief I ended up with in that moment?

To help you put these insights into practice, I've created a free video where you can watch me working with clients to identify and break through their limiting beliefs. If you've already downloaded it, now would be a great time to watch it. You'll find it at www.willsteel.com/freetolead.

CHAPTER TAKEAWAYS

» It is our interpretation, our narrative of the events, not the events themselves, that has the lasting impact on our lives and defines the way we show up in our world.

» Over time, we gather 'evidence' that reinforces these beliefs, making them even stronger.

» When we can learn to separate out the events from the decisions we made, we can free ourselves from the limiting beliefs we previously formed.

Chapter 5

DISCOVERING WHO YOU REALLY ARE

'Who you really are is way more than you could ever imagine.'

If I asked you who you are, to describe your true self, would you be able to? Most people would struggle to answer that question with any certainty. You could start with your name. But that's just a word someone decided to call you. Maybe you are your profession—an engineer. But that's not who you are; that's what you do in life. Or maybe 'I'm an Englishman, that's who I am.' That's where you were born. It's not *who* you are. When you continue in this way, ultimately, where you'll get to is, *I don't know.* **I'd like you to consider that who you really are is way more than you could ever imagine.**

No matter how successful you are, who you have become in life is a limited, compartmentalised version of who you really are, constrained by the limiting beliefs and decisions you have made as you have gone through life. So, how do you become the full, free version of yourself? How do you really know who you are? What does the 'real you' even mean?

The real you is not about the physical. You are not your body. While you have a body and you need it to be alive, you are not defined by it. Imagine if you lost an arm. You would still be you—just without that arm.

The real you is also not about your thoughts. Your thoughts aren't always based on reality. They are automatic, reactionary—and they are not who you are. We all have a constant stream of thoughts running through our minds, often without our control. And this inner dialogue is often influenced by the stories we tell ourselves—in Chapter 4, we unpacked some of this.

The ongoing conversation in our heads can be negative and self-deprecating. For instance, you might think, 'Will I ever be happy?' or 'Will I ever be successful?' But these are just thoughts—not you. They are automatic and subconscious. They are mostly in our own voice, so we really feel like we are creating them, that they *are* us. But that's the illusion of being human. We are conned by our brain to believe that the thoughts we are having are us. Consider that thoughts are just thoughts. How many times have you had the same thoughts over and over again? It's been happening your whole life. You may ask yourself, 'How can it not be me? It's me talking, isn't it?' Well, have you ever had an argument with yourself? One minute, you are one voice, and the next, you're arguing the other point of view. Interesting, isn't it?

However, if we don't see our thoughts, especially of the negative self-talk variety, for what they are— just thoughts— they shape us. They impact how we see ourselves and how we interact with the world. If you constantly tell yourself that you are not good enough, you will start to believe it. You will act in ways that reinforce this belief, limiting your potential. For example, you might avoid applying for new positions, starting a business, or asking for a promotion—all because you don't truly believe you can succeed. This is how negative self-talk becomes a self-fulfilling prophecy.

So if you're not your thoughts, then who are you? Your feelings and emotions? Let's take a look at that. You have feelings and emotions, but are they really you? Many people do identify with their emotions and feelings. They say things like, 'I'm sad' or 'I'm anxious,' which is very different from 'I'm feeling sadness in my stomach' or 'I feel anxiousness in my chest.' Although subtle, the former statements identify you *as* the feelings and emotions, and the latter statements distinguish the feelings and emotions as something you have. You are not them (I'll explore this difference further in the next chapter).

So, if you are not your body, your thoughts, or your feelings, who are you really? You may have identified with the way you look, the colour of your skin, your ethnic background, your religious beliefs, or even the kind of music you like, 'I'm a rocker' or 'I'm a rapper.' These are aspects of your life and potentially very important ones. But consider that these are also not who you really are. The real you is not limited by thoughts, feelings, emotions, or any of these attributes.

At the end of this chapter, I will walk you through an exercise that will help you separate the extraneous pieces from who you really are so you can start to uncover the real you. But first, I want to share a story about my own past interpretation of who I was.

WHAT YOU BELIEVE ABOUT YOURSELF VS. WHAT OTHERS SEE

In the first week of my university year, I was lucky enough to encounter the Royal Air Force University Air Squadron at the Freshers' Fair. The guy at the desk told me I could join and get free flying for two years with no long-term commitment to joining the RAF. I wasn't what I thought of as a 'military type.' In fact, I had none of what I thought you would need to be accepted into the military.

I asked the young man, 'So, do you really think I could get in?' 'Sure,' he said. 'Just take your earring out and maybe get a haircut. I'm sure you'll have no trouble.' I was not convinced, but I filled out the application anyway.

To my shock, a letter arrived a few days later asking me to attend an interview. I took out my earring, had a haircut, and went along to the squadron building, where I sat in front of the Squadron Commander and two instructors. They were quite enthusiastic, asking me several questions about my family and my life to date.

I told them that I had not arrived at university via the traditional route. I had no A levels. Instead, I had completed a Technician's Apprenticeship as an engineer and managed to get into university through their interview process. As I told them about myself, I was convinced that they would think of me as less than their normal applicant and not want me. To make matters worse, they pointed to a painting on the wall and asked me what type of aircraft it was. I had no clue. I'd never even considered being a pilot. I had no background knowledge or previous interest in aviation.

I was sure I would be rejected. And yet, I was accepted into the Liverpool University Air Squadron. I was in disbelief. I could not believe I was actually going to be allowed to fly an aeroplane.

They told me I would need a blazer and slacks for the Officer's Mess. I had never owned a suit. So, on the 3rd of January 1986, I drove to RAF Woodvale in my beat-up *Vauxhall Viva*, stopping at a charity shop along the way to pick up a blazer for 50 pence. It all seemed quite surreal.

Within an hour of arriving at the airfield, I was suited up in a flying kit, an oversized helmet, and strapped into a *Bulldog* aeroplane by my instructor, Squadron Leader Kevin Lawry (The Boss). Before I knew it, we were airborne. We flew around, doing some aerobatics. Then he let me take the controls. With small movements of my hand, the aeroplane rolled all the way to the right and then all the way to the left. That was it! I was hooked. I now wanted this more than anything. I was determined to be the best pilot there was.

To my surprise, I later discovered that I was in fact, the first choice of all applicants. Instead of viewing me as less because of my untraditional path to university, The Boss was impressed with my humble beginnings. He found it admirable that I had worked hard and studied at night school to get myself into university. *What I had believed was a deficit was actually what set me apart.*

What I didn't realise is that what I believed about myself wasn't who I was to others; it wasn't an accurate representation, just as what you believe about yourself might not be accurate. It isn't who you really are. Consider it's just a possible interpretation.

Your beliefs about who you are can limit you from being the true you. They might lead you to hold back or make choices out of fear of how others will see you. But the real you is full of potential. My goal is to help you let go of what is holding you back so you can become the real you—the limitless you.

My 27 years of experience working with people all over the world has allowed me to develop this framework that I am about to share with you, so that you too, will have the opportunity to identify what you've believed about yourself, which is often below your level of consciousness. This will enable you to shatter your limiting beliefs and become your true self, living and leading from fittra.

EXERCISE: DISCOVERING THE REAL YOU

To begin discovering who you really are, it's essential to identify and understand the interpretations and decisions that have shaped your life.

Starting on a clean sheet of paper in your notebook, work through the following steps:

Step 1: Who Am I?
List out everything you would typically use to identify yourself and the things you tell yourself about who you are, and what you think others would say if asked to describe you. Keep going until there's nothing left to write.

Step 2: Determine What Doesn't Belong
Look back at the beginning of this chapter and think about whether the things you've written are actually part of your true, deep self. Cross out anything based on physical appearance,

feelings, or emotions. Also, cross out any thoughts you can recognise as automatic opinions—things that are not really you but that you've come to relate to. (I don't think I'm capable, or I could be better, etc.)

Step 3: Reflect On the Real You
Answer the following questions in your notebook:

1. When do you feel most authentically you or at peace in your life?
2. What would you do if you knew you never had to worry about money, 'success', or what anyone else thought about you?
3. What was one time in your childhood when you felt truly happy, free, and enjoying the moment?
4. What is something you want to do or try but have been too afraid to or you talked yourself out of it?

Step 4: Identify Moments Where Limiting Beliefs Were Formed
Based on the answer to the last question, think about where the fears that are holding you back came from or when you first started to believe the things you tell yourself (just like I discovered about my three-year-old self and my decision to prove I was the best. Hearing my parents talk about wanting a girl was the earliest time I remember thinking that in my life). If nothing comes to mind, get in touch with how those fears and thoughts make you feel. Focus on the feeling, and ask yourself 'What does this feeling remind me of from my past?' Just let whatever memory surfaces come all the way up.

Step 5: Challenge Your Early Conclusions

Once you see an early event from your past, ask yourself, 'What did I make that mean? What did I decide?' Write down what you see. Review what you wrote and ask yourself if that is really true, or is it just one possible interpretation?

Step 6: Dwell in The Emotional Weight

Dwell in and connect with the emotional weight these interpretations have had on your life.

Step 7: Create a New Interpretation

Next, work through the 'Rewriting the Narrative' Exercise from Chapter 4 to create a new interpretation. Basically, as you break away from the limiting beliefs shaping you, write out a more empowering interpretation of who you are and what is most important to you. Write this down and keep it where you can see it daily. Doing this will empower you to open up and begin to live as this creation versus repeating your past patterns.

If possible, reach out to an accountability partner, such as a qualified coach, and share this new interpretation—the new *you* that you are committed to being. Schedule regular check-ins to evaluate whether you're showing up authentically as this created you.

REFLECTION QUESTIONS

1. How have my limiting beliefs shaped who I identify as?
2. Am I living life as my true, full self?
3. What decisions in my past have shaped the way I am today?

CHAPTER TAKEAWAYS

» You are not defined by your body, thoughts, or feelings; you are much more than these. Who you are is much bigger than the sum of your parts.

» Many of our beliefs about ourselves are formed in childhood and can limit us.

» The real you isn't limited by negative beliefs, your position in life, or the choices you have made so far. The real you is limitless.

Chapter 6

EMOTIONAL FREEDOM

'When you allow your negative emotions to drive your actions, you are not in control. You are not living from your true self, in fittra.'

Do you find yourself sometimes consumed by negative emotions such as worry, anxiety, guilt, loneliness, jealousy, greed, or anger? Our emotions can become very powerful, dictating our choices and sending us down paths we don't even realise we're taking. But to live authentically in fittra, we must understand our negative emotions—and more specifically, where they come from.

What you might not realise is that your feelings and emotions match your subconscious limiting beliefs. For example, if you believe that the world is an unsafe place, you will experience fear. If you believe that you are not talented, you will experience self-doubt and anxiety prior to any performance.

These beliefs and emotions change the way you act and influence the decisions you make, further confirming your limiting beliefs. For example, if you fear the world is dangerous, you will avoid taking risks in order to keep yourself safe. You might then feel safe because you avoided the risk, but this action only reinforces your belief that the world is dangerous. If you struggle with self-doubt, you're likely to overlook opportunities for growth and learning, convincing yourself that you simply *can't* do them. As a result, you won't develop certain skills or talents, which will prevent you from accomplishing what you are truly capable of. This behaviour unwittingly provides more evidence that your limiting beliefs are true, reinforcing them. This is the trap.

When your negative emotions drive your actions, you are not in control. You are not making conscious decisions. You are not working towards your true desires or living from your true self, in fittra. Instead, you are falling into patterns fueled by decisions you made in the past that became your reality.

In this chapter, you will learn how to see your negative emotions for what they truly are so that you can release their power over you. This is known as emotional freedom.

First, however, you need to understand what feelings and emotions really are so you can learn to respond consciously rather than simply automatically reacting to them.

UNDERSTANDING FEELINGS AND EMOTIONS

We often think of feelings and emotions as the same thing, but there is a difference. Feelings are the *physical* sensations in your body, like a tightness in your chest or a sinking feeling in your stomach. Emotions, on the other hand, are the *mental* interpretations of these sensations. For instance, a tightness in your chest could be interpreted as anxiety or excitement, depending on the context. Understanding this distinction is crucial because it helps you see that your emotions are not fixed; they are shaped by the thoughts and interpretations that you give significance to.

THE BRAIN'S JOB

Your brain is the driving force behind this process. Its primary job is to keep you alive by continuously scanning your environment for threats and opportunities. When it detects a threat, it immediately triggers an emotional response to prepare you for action, even before you consciously recognise the danger. For example, if you see a snake, your brain primes you to react with fear, preparing you to run, freeze, or fight, often within 50 milliseconds, before you've fully recognised that what's in front of you is a snake.

The brain's ability to create emotional responses is a survival mechanism. However, it can also work against you.

The amygdala is a small almond-shaped structure in the brain with a big job. It is responsible for detecting threats, initiating the fight-or-flight response, processing emotions, forming memories, and assigning emotional significance to sensory information.

When you encounter a situation that triggers an emotional response, the amygdala sends signals to other parts of the brain, including the prefrontal cortex, which is responsible for decision-making and rational thought. If the emotional response is strong enough, the amygdala can override the prefrontal cortex, leading to impulsive or irrational behaviour. Have you ever seen a police car in your car mirror and felt panicked despite knowing that you were driving safely and legally? That's one example of how your brain can override rational thought.

Your brain forms emotional patterns, often without you realising it. For instance, if your brain learns that becoming upset helps you get what you want, it will continue to trigger that response in similar situations. This happens because your brain knows you can survive those emotions, and it seeks familiarity. Without realising it, at a subconscious level, you may even orchestrate situations in your life to repeat these familiar patterns.

Perhaps your relationships always follow the same troubled path and never work out. Maybe you get close to success at work only to fail at the last hurdle time and time again. Or perhaps you find yourself getting upset over trivial things. These patterns are not random. They are the result of deep-seated beliefs and emotional responses that your brain has programmed into you.

FALLING INTO A PATTERN OF NEGATIVE EMOTIONS

We often don't realise the negative patterns we fall into. This is something I experienced when in flight school. On my first flight assessment, I scored 74, which was the second highest in the squadron that year. The examiner told me, 'If you'd have been one of those who suffer from testitis (test anxiety), I wouldn't have knocked off so many marks at the beginning.'

Hoping he would adjust my score, I said, 'Oh, I do get nervous.' He didn't adjust my score. And this statement would come to haunt me. As I took more and more flying tests, I actually became more and more nervous. In fact, it became so intense that it almost cost me my flying career. I would start feeling anxious the moment I saw a test in my schedule. I secretly believed I wasn't as good as I seemed to be, even though I had evidence to the contrary. (I had even won aerobatics and low-level fast jet navigation trophies as I went through my training.)

It wasn't until years later, after applying the lessons in this book, that I dismantled my fear of flying tests and tests in general. I had made it up, trying to get sympathy, but it grew into a fear that escalated and caused me years of anxiety.

Our limiting beliefs often begin with small incidents, but they can sink deep into the subconscious and gradually take control of our lives as we accumulate more and more evidence to support them.

My fear drove me and controlled me. It held me back from opportunities and led me into self-sabotage. It wasn't until I learned to recognise the patterns I was falling into, identify the emotions I was experiencing, and rewrite the beliefs that fueled them, that I was able to break free. That's emotional freedom—and why it's so important. As long as we allow ourselves to be controlled by negative emotions, we remain tethered to our limiting beliefs and past narratives.

ACHIEVING EMOTIONAL FREEDOM

I've already shared examples of how your negative emotions can affect your choices. According to my friend, Dr. Ahmed Eldemellawy, emotions are also the source of illness and disease in the body. Emotions like stress, anxiety, and fear can have a profound impact on your physical health. When you hold on to negative emotions, they can manifest as physical symptoms or even chronic conditions.

Emotional freedom occurs when you see these negative emotions for what they are, identify the thoughts that trigger them to begin with, and not only create new narratives, but release the stored emotions from your body. This allows you to break the negative patterns you are stuck in.

To gain emotional freedom, start by recognising the familiar emotions and feelings you experience. Begin to inquire when these particular feelings and emotions started to occur in your life. Ask yourself, 'What does this feeling or emotion remind me of from my past?' This question can help you uncover the root cause of your emotional responses. For example, I had to trace my test anxiety back to the moment I told my instructor that I had been nervous on my flight test. When I uncovered that source, I was able to rewrite the narrative and break out of the pattern.

REGULATING YOUR EMOTIONAL RESPONSE

Once you identify the source of your own negative emotions, you can begin to regulate those responses. Two effective techniques can help you—mindfulness and cognitive restructuring. Mindfulness involves paying attention to your thoughts and feelings without judgement. By observing your emotions without getting caught up in them, you can create a pause—a space between the stimulus and your response. This allows you to choose how you want to react rather than being controlled by your emotions.

At first, mindfulness can feel difficult. But the more you practise, the easier it becomes. It can be helpful to start using mindfulness outside of emotional moments where the stakes don't seem as high. Try setting aside a few minutes each day to sit quietly and focus on your breath, noticing each inhale and exhale. If your mind wanders, gently bring your attention back to your breathing.

You can also incorporate mindfulness into daily activities by paying attention to simple moments. For example, while on a walk, instead of letting your mind wander to other things, focus on what you see and feel around you and the sensation of your movements, staying in the moment. Even a few mindful moments a day, practised consistently, can build these skills and make it easier to create that pause when you start to experience negative emotions. You can make a conscious decision in place of the automatic response.

Cognitive restructuring is the process of challenging and changing negative thought patterns. For example, if you catch yourself thinking you're not good enough, ask yourself if that thought is really true. Look for evidence to the contrary and reframe the thought in a more positive light: 'I am enough exactly as I am' or 'I have accomplished many things and am capable of doing even more.' Over time, this can shift your emotional responses and create new, healthier patterns.

For example, as I shared in Chapter 4, I carried a deep-seated belief that I was not wanted by my parents. This belief had shaped my entire life, leading me to strive for success while never feeling truly satisfied. But by confronting and challenging this belief, I was able to start dismantling the emotional responses that came with it. This process wasn't easy, and it took time, but it was incredibly freeing—it allowed me to regain control over my emotions and to break negative patterns of thought and behaviour.

As you develop these skills, you will start to recognise your emotions and identify the thoughts and beliefs that shape them. From there, you will be able to respond from a place of choice rather than automatic reaction, breaking your old patterns.

EXERCISE: REFRAMING NEGATIVE EMOTIONS

Identifying recurring emotions can help lead you to moments in your past where limiting beliefs were formed. Using the strategies found earlier in this book, along with what you've learned in this chapter, you can reframe those interpretations and start to build emotional freedom.

To begin, turn to a blank page in your notebook and divide it into five columns. Label them as below:

Identify Recurring Emotions	Explore the Source	Identify the Interpretation	Gather Opposing Evidence	New Interpretation

Under each column, use the guide below to help you write in your responses.

Identify Recurring Emotions

List the negative emotions you find yourself experiencing repeatedly, such as jealousy or anger. It can be helpful to explore this over a few days, noticing what comes up and what triggers each one. You can also look at how familiar these are and how long you have been experiencing them as you have gone through life.

Explore the Source

What earlier events or experiences do those emotions remind you of from your past? Write these down. See if you can get back to the very earliest time you experienced them.

Identify the Interpretation

What beliefs or interpretations did you form in those early moments?

Gather Evidence

Was your interpretation true, or was it a story you told yourself? What evidence do you have that contradicts that interpretation?

New Interpretation

Create a new, more empowering interpretation of the events at the source of your negative emotions. (Revisit Chapter 4 on The Stories We Tell Ourselves if needed.)

REFLECTION QUESTIONS

1. Do I find myself getting upset easily or frequently reacting in familiar ways? (For example, do I get upset when things don't go my way?)
2. When these emotions show up, what do I feel in my body, and where?
3. What experiences from my past do these emotions remind me of?
4. What did I decide in those moments?

CHAPTER TAKEAWAYS

» Your feelings and emotions are often automatic responses based on limiting beliefs.

» Identifying and challenging these emotional patterns can allow you to respond with choice rather than automatic reactions.

» You can gain emotional freedom by seeing your automatic emotional responses for what they are and getting to the source of them.

Chapter 7

Overcoming Fear
and Anxiety

*'Our fears may feel very real, but they often
stem from our past experiences and the
interpretations we've made.'*

In the last chapter, we discussed the way negative emotions can shape the way we show up in life. But there is one emotion that is particularly strong, and it needs its own chapter—*fear*. Most of us are walking through life experiencing some level of fear, whether we realise it or not. And the worst part is we get so used to it that we hardly notice it.

In many cases, we don't realise that it's fear we're really experiencing. After all, fear isn't just the palpable, heart-beating kind. More often, our fear is subtle and insidious. Fears can materialise as doubt, questioning oneself, procrastination, distraction, laziness, and perfectionism, to name a few. If we dig even deeper, usually, there are also strong, emotional fears that rumble below the surface —like the fear of being found out that you're not good enough or the fear of vulnerability or intimacy.

Fear often lies beneath the surface, dictating our choices in life and keeping us in automatic patterns, just like the other negative emotions we discussed in Chapter 6.

Until we learn how to identify our fears and overcome them, we will continue to fall into the related negative patterns. The good news is that when you can trace back your fears and identify the limiting beliefs at play, you can see fear for what it is, release its power over you, and make decisions not from fear but from your true self, your fittra.

UNDERSTANDING AND OVERCOMING FEAR

Most of what we are afraid of doesn't really exist. Authentic fear arises from immediate physical threats, like a dangerous animal in the wild, an out-of-control car hurtling towards you, or a mugger with a knife attacking you, etc. However, many fears are psychological—based on imagined outcomes rather than present dangers. We are trying to avoid what we *believe* might happen. This can result in anxiety or hypervigilance, where we become overly alert and worried about bad things happening making it difficult to relax or sleep.

To overcome fear and anxiety, it's crucial to distinguish real threats from imagined ones. Real threats require immediate action for safety, while imagined threats can be tackled by using the exercise that follows shortly.

Fear often originates from the tendency of our minds to anticipate negative outcomes. This anticipation is a mental trap that can paralyse us and prevent us from taking action. For example, you might worry about a difficult conversation with a colleague, fearing conflict or rejection. This fear isn't based on reality but rather on what *might happen*, driven by past experiences of similar situations. Fear might arise before an important business meeting or a tough conversation with an employee, asking someone in your life to help you, or even asking someone out on a date. In all of these situations, there is no real threat to your physical survival—but the experience can be just as terrifying. Our fears may feel very real, but they often stem from past experiences and the interpretations we've made. The good news is that we have the power to rewrite and reframe them, as we've done throughout the chapters of this book.

As I've already shared, in my own life, I spent much of my career grappling with an underlying fear of not being good enough. This fear was particularly strong when I was evaluated by superiors, as in my earlier example of when I was undergoing a flying test or when I had to perform under pressure. It was a fear rooted in past experiences throughout my childhood, like being told I wasn't meeting expectations or feeling judged for my work. These moments solidified the belief that I was always on the verge of failure, which in turn made me anxious about any situation where my performance was scrutinised.

A breakthrough moment came when I was coaching a group of leaders and felt a wave of fear just before stepping onto the stage. I paused and asked myself, '*What's really going on here?*' I realised that the fear wasn't about actual danger; it was about being judged or failing in front of these people. So I questioned it: '*Is this fear based on what is actually happening now, or something I'm imagining?*' I reminded myself of my purpose—I was here to serve, to make a difference. That shift in focus didn't make the fear disappear completely, but it loosened its grip. I was able to move forward with clarity and energy—and delivered a powerful, successful event for everyone involved.

Even if you have been living in fear for most of your life, you can change the way you move forward. Neuroscience says that the only way to make lasting change is to learn to see yourself and the world differently. If you want to be more confident and authentic, that means no longer letting fear control how you interpret the world. Instead, you can learn to recognise inauthentic fear, separate it from reality, overcome your limiting beliefs—and start to see the world as it actually is. The following exercise will help you begin to identify and overcome your fears.

EXERCISE: IDENTIFYING AND CONQUERING FEAR

Turn to a blank page in your notebook and work through the following steps:

Step 1: Identify the Fear

Write down the fears that frequently arise in your life in everyday situations, like in work meetings, addressing issues in your relationships, people approaching you in the street, speaking up in public, etc. Keep going until you have a complete list. Include even all the little fears. Once you've completed your list, look back over it and pick the fear that impacts you the most. Ask yourself: Is this fear about what's actually happening—or about what I'm imagining might happen?

Step 2: Reflect on Past Experiences

Consider past experiences that may have contributed to your fears. Ask yourself, what does this remind me of? What's the earliest time I remember feeling like this? What was happening? Who was there? Then ask yourself, what decisions did I make in those early moments? Write these down. Now, like we've done in the earlier chapters, question these interpretations by asking these follow-up questions: Did it really mean that? Is that the truth about me and others, or was it just one possible interpretation I made at the time?

For example, when I was working for my last employer, I struggled with a fear of being shouted at or facing disciplinary action—something I had experienced in the past. Once I identified the source of that fear, I realised it was rooted in something much earlier.

When I was young, I would do things I knew I shouldn't, and then the fear would set in—that I'd be in trouble and my father would shout at me. That old pattern was still running in the background. Recognising this helped me detach from the fear. I began asking myself, *'Is there a real threat right now? Is someone actually going to get me?'*

While it didn't completely eliminate the physical symptoms, it allowed me to stay grounded and be more present.

If you can identify where your fears first came from, you are well on the way to breaking the grip that these fears have on you.

Step 3: Commit to Mindfulness

Once you learn to identify your fears for what they are, you will be able to spot them as they arise. When this happens, take a moment to breathe and centre yourself. You can even say, 'Oh, there's my fear,' and just be with it—experience it as it is, let yourself fully feel the sensations. Focus on what is happening in the present moment rather than getting lost in all the possible outcomes of how things might go.

A technique I learned from Christian Mickelsen is called **The Peace Process**. It involves focusing on the physical sensation of fear in your body. Once you locate the most intense sensation, put your index finger on it and try to fully experience the sensation. Every 30 to 60 seconds, ask yourself, 'What's happening in my body now?' Then, locate where the most intense sensation is at that moment because it may have moved. If it has moved, put your index finger on the new location and try to fully experience the sensation as it is in this new moment. If you do this for long enough, you will find the sensation dissipates. Keep doing this until it disappears fully. As the saying goes, 'The more you feel it, the more you heal it.'

Step 4: Take Small Steps

Challenge yourself to take small actions towards the things you fear. This can help build confidence and reduce the power of fear over time. Start with manageable steps, and gradually increase the challenge as you grow more comfortable. Keep reminding yourself that it's just your fear; it's not you. Once you get that it's there, but it doesn't control you, that's when you have an opportunity to let it be and take the action you are afraid of.

For example, I recently tested this to the extreme by doing a bungee jump in Cabo, Mexico. From the very moment

I agreed to do it, I was dealing with waves of fear. As I got closer to the actual jump, this got more and more intense. I was afraid I would even faint and not be allowed to jump. However, by doing The Peace Process repeatedly, I was able to work through my fear—and, on the count of three, jump out into space. Whoa! It was an amazing experience and a testament to the power of doing this exercise.

Remember, if you feel you need any additional support, please head to www.willsteel.com/freetolead.

REFLECTION QUESTIONS

1. What are some common fears I experience?
2. How have these fears held me back?
3. What moments from my past do these fears remind me of?

CHAPTER TAKEAWAYS

» Fear and anxiety often stem from imagined outcomes rather than real threats.

» Learning to identify past situations that are contributing to our imagined threats can help us move past them and take control of our fear.

» When we can recognise our fears and move through them, they lose their power over us.

Chapter 8

BREAKING FREE FROM AUTOMATIC MECHANISMS

'To truly live in fittra, you need to be in the driver's seat of your own life—not going along for the ride, driven by your past and your limiting beliefs.'

In Chapters 6 and 7, I unpacked the way that negative emotions and fear form as an automatic response fueled by limiting beliefs and past narratives. But it isn't only our emotions that become automatic—it's also our actions. In many cases, our actions are actually *reactions*. We react automatically, often without realising exactly what is happening. Whenever you feel attacked or put down in some way, you react. Beneath these reactions are those same limiting beliefs, telling us to protect ourselves, to avoid potentially painful situations, or to prove that we're 'right', to avoid blame, or to hurt others before they hurt us.

Reactions could be overt or covert. You might snap and bite someone's head off, or you might simply feel a little upset and become quiet. However you react, it's a signal that there is something deeper being triggered from your past—a limiting belief is surfacing.

When you react, you aren't just experiencing the moment you are in, you are seeing and hearing through the filters of your limiting beliefs and your brain's automatic interpretations.

For example, perhaps you have become a people-pleaser because, deep down, you believe that other people's needs matter more than yours. Or if you think that you always mess everything up, you might find yourself criticising or blaming yourself when things go wrong without even realising that there is an ongoing pattern at play. Whatever patterns you fall into, you aren't in control when you're reacting. When you feel yourself getting triggered, you might go along with the reaction, or you might try to ignore it and pretend that you are 'fine'. But to truly live in fittra, you need to be in the driver's seat of your own life—not going along for the ride, driven by your past limiting beliefs.

I challenge you to start looking at your reactions as a signal to explore deeper, using the methods you are learning (and will continue to learn) in this book. You could think of it as an archeological dig into your past to uncover hidden treasure—to find the root of your upset that has been activated by the current situation. Once you see the source of your behaviour (your limiting belief), you can begin to break free of the automatic reactions and responses that currently run your life. It takes practice and awareness. But it is possible to stop automatic patterns and replace them with conscious choices.

AUTOMATIC PATTERNS: THE NEED TO BE 'RIGHT'

On my own archaeological dig, I discovered why I spent most of my life resisting anything my father said. I heard almost everything he said as a criticism, as him telling me I was wrong. When he tried to help me or offer advice, I would dismiss it before he had even finished speaking. I would get annoyed and even upset, automatically believing he didn't know what he was talking about. In fact, I would often do the opposite of what he advised.

Eventually, I started working with a coach to break away from my reactions—and I discovered the incident that started this pattern. I remembered sitting at the dinner table when I was eight years old. I told my father something my teacher had told us that day at school. My father said, 'That's not true.'

I was adamant that it was true. My teacher had told me, and I believed him. My father became irate and said, 'Listen to me, I'm your father! Believe what I say. I'm telling you that's not true.' I remember thinking to myself, *'I can't believe what you say. I can't believe what anyone says.'*

This message sank deep into my subconscious. Upon revisiting this incident, I was able to see that I had lived my life not believing what anyone said. I had to verify everything for myself. My first thought when someone tried to tell me anything was the opposite viewpoint from whatever they said. I became an automatic devil's advocate, often becoming argumentative or challenging whatever anyone said. I spent my entire life behaving this way—and I thought it was just the way I was. I was unaware that it all stemmed from the decision I made at eight years old.

(Looking back, I have found myself remembering many things my father said to me over the years. He actually had some really good advice that the younger version of me simply couldn't hear. I rejected his input on autopilot, never stopping to truly understand why.)

My automatic reaction to be 'right' and to prove others wrong is far from rare. It's something that I've seen in countless numbers of people that I have coached. They feel the need to defend their point of view, opinion, a belief they hold dear, an image they have of themselves, or some moral standpoint.

You are likely the same. Think about the way you react when others disagree with your opinion or challenge your perspective. You don't just have an opinion—you *are* your opinion, and you have to defend it. That's why changing someone's mind is one of the hardest things to do.

Human beings would rather die than be wrong, or to look at it a different way, they would die for what they see as right. People are wired to be 'right' and, as a result, often feel the need to prove others wrong. They feel justified, in doing so, even at the expense of their relationship with others. It's not until people see the damage of clinging on to being right that they might begin to let go. Even then, it's rare for human beings to be willing to let go of having to prove they are right unless they are working with a qualified coach who can skillfully point out the consequences of holding onto this, without further threatening their identity or moral standpoint they are defending. The benefits of this work are extremely rewarding. Consider, even if you are right, there's little to be gained from *being right* that you are right. Making others wrong damages your relationship with them.

When I was able to see where my automatic reaction started from and did the work to let go of that need to be right, it was like a weight was lifted off of my shoulders. I discovered that it was no big deal to let go of my opinion of the truth and consider others' opinions as a possible way to look at things. As a result, I was able to relax and not be so defensive, making me easier to interact with.

Imagine being a leader that has to be right, who argues and gets defensive when others have a contrary view or a different idea. That's not an environment for creativity and contribution. By learning to master your reactions and encourage others to contribute their ideas, you will elevate your leadership, and people will be more motivated to work with and for you.

ANOTHER COMMON AUTOMATIC REACTION: THE BLAME GAME

One of the other common automatic mechanisms I find with so many of the people I coach is the blame game. Think about an argument you might have had with a romantic partner. If they expressed a concern about something you did, what was your first reaction? Was it to take accountability or listen to their perspective? Or was it to turn it around and pin the blame on them?

We can turn defensive and play the blame game, not just in romantic relationships, but in any area of life. We might blame others for our circumstances, for our feelings, or even for our actions. Think about a time when you have done this. Perhaps you received a reprimand at work and later fumed and vented over what a terrible boss you had. Or maybe you find yourself blaming others for your financial situation or for not receiving a promotion.

When we blame others or the circumstances, we give our power away to something outside of ourselves.

When you blame others, you are saying that they are responsible for your feelings, your situation, and your life. This perspective leaves you powerless and unable to change your circumstances. But when you take responsibility for everything in your life, you are putting yourself at the source of your life—you're not the victim of anything outside of yourself. Now, this may be a hard pill to swallow. And I'm not saying that it is always the truth. However, by adopting this perspective, you will shed the feelings of being a victim and start to experience real power in your life.

Owning your part in what's happening puts you back in the driver's seat. But that doesn't mean you ought to blame yourself. There's a big difference between blame and ownership.

I'm not making myself wrong when I say, *'This is mine to look at.'* I'm recognising that I have the power to shift it. I'm acknowledging that I am the one creating my life. I'm not going to blame others for my experience.

For example, if my team fails to produce an outcome we set out to produce, rather than blame the team members for not doing what they should have done, I stand in, *'Oh they did that because I didn't explain, emphasise, or manage that they carried out the actions effectively to produce the desired result.'*

This doesn't mean you shouldn't hold others to account for doing their job—that would be irresponsible. But, by taking responsibility for your part, it gives you the power to improve the situation.

FORMING A CONSCIOUS RESPONSE

When you start to see the automatic patterns and reactions you have, such as blaming others or instantly dismissing advice, you have the opportunity to make a shift. You can recognise your patterns at play and consciously respond in a different way. For example, instead of immediately rejecting someone's suggestion that is different from what you are proposing, you could say something like, 'Hmm, wait a minute, let me look at that for a moment. Say more about why you think that... ' Even if you ultimately believe your idea is better and decide not to change your plan, the person making the suggestion will feel heard and appreciated. This creates an environment where they are more likely to continue contributing their ideas in the future. Ultimately, this approach fosters a team that feels involved in the decision-making process, which is empowering for those you lead.

EXERCISE: BREAKING AWAY FROM AUTOMATIC MECHANISMS

Work through this exercise on a blank sheet of paper in your notebook:

Step 1: Identify Automatic Reactions
Over the next week, pay attention to your reactions in challenging situations. Write down instances where you felt defensive, angry, upset, or found yourself placing blame on others. Note what triggered these reactions.

Step 2: Explore the Source

Once you have started to identify your automatic reactions, reflect on what those reactions remind you of from your past, tracing them back to the earliest moments you can remember feeling that way. Write down these experiences and the interpretations you made at the time. (Revisit the exercise Rewriting Your Stories from Chapter 4 if needed.)

Step 3: Create a New Response

Create a new, more empowering response that you can choose in place of your automatic reaction. While the automatic reaction may still occur, recognising it allows you to see these responses as habitual. One empowering response you could adopt is to pause and take a few deep breaths before speaking or acting. Alternatively, you might pause and count to 10 before saying anything, or create a practice of your own, then remind yourself, 'Even though I feel the urge to react, I'm choosing not to.'

Step 4: Take Responsibility

Examine how you can take responsibility for what's happening. Ask yourself, 'What can I take responsibility for here?' To deepen your sense of responsibility, consider what the current reaction may be reminding you of from your past and counter it with a supportive thought. For example, you might remind yourself, 'No one is attacking me right now' or 'They're not calling me stupid.'

Example

Identify the Automatic Reaction	Explore the Source	Create a New Response
I feel the automatic need to counter and argue against any point of view.	When my father disagreed with my teacher and told me to believe him instead, I told myself that I couldn't believe what anyone said.	When presented with new information, ask a question to learn more and discover where the other person is coming from, rather than being combative.

REFLECTION QUESTIONS

1. What are some familiar automatic reactions I often experience?
2. How have these automatic reactions impacted my life or my relationships?
3. With each automatic reaction you identify, ask yourself, 'What is the earliest time I remember feeling like this?' and 'What was happening at the time?'

CHAPTER TAKEAWAYS:

» Automatic reactions often stem from past experiences and limiting beliefs.

» We often blame others or try to prove our 'rightness' through repeated patterns without realising it.

» By becoming aware of these patterns, we can take responsibility and choose our responses, creating the life we want rather than being at the effect of our circumstances and automatic reactions.

Chapter 9

STRATEGIES FOR SUCCESS

'Success gained from trying to prove yourself to yourself will never be enough. It will always leave you feeling empty.'

Many of the world's most 'successful' people have everything on the outside—money, recognition, status—but still feel an emptiness inside. They're not fulfilled. No matter how much they achieve, it never quite feels like enough.

If you've ever hit a major goal and found yourself thinking, 'Now what?' or 'Why doesn't this feel the way I thought it would?'—you're not alone.

I remember getting my fast jet pilot wings after years of pushing, striving, sacrificing—doing whatever it took. And when I finally got them, I looked around and saw everyone else wearing the same wings. It was meant to be a moment of pride, of triumph... but it didn't land like that. It didn't feel special. It felt flat.

I was actually disappointed. After everything I'd been through, it didn't feel the way I thought it would. I still didn't feel like a real pilot—not really. I had the badge but not the feeling I thought it would give me.

I still didn't feel good enough.

And that's the pattern for so many of us. Most of us have developed personal success strategies—ways we push, prove, and achieve—not from our true selves in fittra, but as a way to cope with early experiences of not feeling good enough.

Psychologists call these patterns of behaviour, developed to help us feel safe, worthy, or significant, compensatory strategies. They often work, and they can produce real results. But they're not rooted in your true self. They're rooted in a moment from your past when you decided who you needed to be in order to survive, belong, or win.

In my case, I would set big targets for myself—like getting into university or becoming a fast jet pilot. But the moment I accomplished the goals, it wasn't long before I'd be looking around, asking, '*Now what? What's the next big thing to go for?*' No matter what I achieved, it was never enough.

Does this sound familiar to you too?

My need to be the best and prove myself—that was my first strategy for success.

Success is often measured by what we achieve—the goals we hit, the results we produce. And when we do hit those goals, it feels good… for a while. But that feeling rarely lasts.

That's because these strategies weren't born from your true self. They were formed in moments when you felt like you weren't enough.

This isn't just your story—it's a human phenomenon. We all create ways to succeed that are designed not from wholeness, but from compensation.

As you read on, I'll show you how this gets set up and how to recognise your own success strategies and where they began. This awareness is powerful. Without it, you'll produce results but never truly feel fulfilled or at peace with what you accomplish.

Rick Rubin, the legendary music producer, worked with countless well-known artists before finally landing a number-one album with the Beastie Boys. When asked how he felt, he said it was the saddest he had ever been. He had achieved the external success he'd been chasing—but it didn't bring him happiness.

He went on to say he'd seen the same thing in many artists: They spend years trying to create a hit, only to find that when they finally do, nothing really *changes* inside.

That's the trap—external results don't shift how you feel about yourself.

But you can break out of the endless striving. Once you begin to heal, you realise you don't have to prove anything. You don't need to hit goals to feel okay with who you are.

And that doesn't mean you stop producing results. It means the results you create start coming from who you truly are—an authentic expression of yourself and what really matters to you.

FROM UNWANTED TO UNFULFILLED

In my case, if you remember, when I was three years old, and I heard my father say they hadn't planned a baby and they were looking forward to a little girl, I declared, 'I'm the best.' From that moment forward, my life became about proving that I was the best. However, whenever I accomplished being the best at something, it didn't fix that feeling inside of not being enough. No matter what external results I produced, it didn't fill this void. Nothing ever felt like enough.

When I was eleven, I started secondary school in Yorkshire. My older brothers spent the summer before telling me horror stories about what happened to new first-year students on the first day of term. The older boys would rip off the tabs on the back of the first-year boys' ties or stuff 'First Years' into waste baskets and roll them around the playground. Another tradition was that there would always be a fight on the first day of school to determine the 'Cock of the First Years' (the toughest boy). It was decided that this fight would be between me and Conrad Zatorski, a Polish boy built like a brick outhouse.

Inside, I was scared—but I couldn't let it show. My father, who had been a boxer, had often said, 'Never let them know you're scared. Avoid fights if you can, but if you have to fight, get the first punch in so they don't think you're scared of them. A fight can be won with the first punch. And if you do get into a fight, go absolutely crazy, so that anyone watching won't think of ever trying it on with you.'

(I now know my father wanted the best for me. He had been brought up in a tough time where there was little to no support from parents. If you got into a fight or were bullied, you were on your own. He took up boxing to learn how to survive the harsh reality of his surroundings. In his world, there was no one to protect him. He had to learn to defend himself. So he had been giving me his advice about having to be tough all my life.)

As the first day of school came near, and the fight that I believed was waiting for me approached, my father's words rang in my ears over and over. Finally, the day arrived. As I headed out to the playground for the first recess, my heart was in my mouth. I envisioned a gladiator scene. I was scared but couldn't let anybody know—I didn't want anyone to see me as weak.

Suddenly, Conrad's friend burst through the doors and, waving his arms, proclaimed, 'You win. Conrad doesn't want to fight. He was almost too scared to come to school, so you win. Alright?'

I calmly said, 'Okay.' And off he scampered.

I didn't have to fight. But instead of feeling relieved, my mind went crazy. I had a problem now— everyone was going to think I was tough—they didn't know how scared I had been. After that, I believed that I had to make sure no one ever found out that I wasn't as tough as they thought; otherwise, I would surely get beaten up. From this moment on, I became super aware of whatever was happening around me, looking out for any potential trouble before it began.

I spent the next five years avoiding trouble and acting tough, so no one would think they had a chance of beating me up. I became super vigilant, always calculating my next move. I also became secretive, careful never to reveal how I really felt—because I was scared that anything I said might make me look weak. This became my strategy for 'success'. And it worked. It got me through. But it never fixed that feeling underneath of not feeling as tough as I wanted people to believe I was.

This way of thinking and acting carried forward into the rest of my life. I always tried to figure out if others were out to get me. I lived in my mind; I couldn't stop. During conversations, I would think two to three steps ahead. As a result, I was never actually present in the moment. I was never relaxed. I was always experiencing a threat, especially from authority.

It wasn't until my coach pointed it out to me, while I was training to lead transformational programs, that I realised how badly I needed to break this pattern. How could I listen and be present enough to coach participants if I was stuck in my head, worrying about whether they were going to try to spoil the course, make me look stupid, or ultimately have me fail to lead a successful program?

It took about two years to train myself out of this automatic behaviour—and I still have to be aware when I default to being in my mind and not present in conversations. It's important to remember that even when you do this work, there will be moments when you find yourself falling into default patterns. You need to learn to identify when this happens so you can correct yourself, let the *automatic* you go, and bring forward your *authentic* self, the self you are committed to being, in fittra.

Another strategy I relied on to produce results was working hard—relentlessly. I could pull all-nighters without hesitation to meet a deadline. I thought it was just who I was, and I was proud of it. But over time, working hard became my answer to everything... and I started burning out. It wasn't until I did the work to reveal the hidden limiting belief that fueled this way of being that I had access to anything else. I was a one gear machine when it came to producing results. Here's what I discovered for myself.

When I was 11 years old, and just starting my new school, there was a boy in my class called Robert Tyce. He knew all the answers to the teacher's questions. He already spoke French, could play the violin perfectly, and just seemed to know everything. I remember looking across the classroom at him and thinking, *'I'm not like him. I'm not academic.'* That was the moment I gave up on studies. I thought I had no chance against people like him who just understood everything straight away. I was not smart that way. These beliefs for me were real. I truly believed I was not academically smart.

Consequently I left school at 16 years old and started work as an engineering apprentice. Two weeks into the job I remember looking at my hands and saw they were dirty. I said to myself, 'I have really screwed up. I'm going to have dirty hands for the rest of my life. I'm not like all those smart kids that stayed on at school. But I am going to get on. I'm going to work really hard.' And I did. I enrolled at night school and studied in addition to my apprenticeship so that I could be considered for university through their interview scheme. It worked; I got into Liverpool University. However, even though I graduated with an Honors Degree in Electronic Engineering, I didn't feel like I was actually smart. I had just worked hard. This shows how even when your strategies produce results, they still don't bring real fulfillment. It's as though you are a fraud. It's as though every time you produce results from your strategies it reminds you of what you believe you are not. This is why, even if your strategies do bring you success, they will never bring you peace, satisfaction, and fulfillment.

These strategies got me through. They helped me survive, perform, and even succeed on the outside. But they never gave me peace. That's the thing about these patterns: they keep producing results, but they also keep you disconnected from who you really are.

And this isn't just about me. We've all built strategies to cope, to fit in, to avoid being hurt, or to prove something. But if you keep living inside them, you'll keep reinforcing the very beliefs you're trying to escape.

So now it's your turn.

Let's uncover the strategies you've been relying on—and the limiting beliefs that shaped them. The following exercise will help you begin that process.

EXERCISE: IDENTIFYING YOUR STRATEGIES FOR SUCCESS (AND WHAT THEY'RE COSTING YOU)

Use a blank sheet in your notebook and work through the steps below to uncover the strategies for success you've been using—and the limiting beliefs that have been driving them.

Step 1: What's Been Driving You?

Think about what success has meant to you over the years. What were you really chasing? What did you believe you had to achieve to finally feel enough?

Now go deeper. What was your *battle cry*?

Was it something like:

- 'I'll prove I'm good enough.'
- 'I'll show them I'm not a failure.'
- 'I'm going to be the best.'
- 'No one's ever going to hurt me again.'
- 'I'll do it all on my own.'
- 'I'll be the one who makes it.'
- 'I'm gonna win.'
- 'I'll never be poor.'
- 'I'll earn their respect.'

What was the fuel behind your drive?

Write down any key phrases, beliefs, or inner declarations that shaped the way you've gone after success. Don't worry if they sound extreme—they often started as childhood decisions made in moments of pain, fear, or defiance.

This is the beginning of uncovering your personal strategy for success.

Step 2: Identify the Origin
Think back to specific moments in your life when you felt lacking in some way—like you weren't enough, didn't belong, or needed to prove something.

What happened? What did you feel? Write down the events and the context around them.

Step 3: Identify the Belief
For each of those moments, what did you tell yourself about you, others, or the world?

Examples:

- 'I'm not smart.'
- 'I'm not as good.'

- 'I'm not enough.'
- 'I have to take care of everyone.'
- 'No one will ever choose me.'
- 'I'm only valuable if I succeed.'
- 'They don't love me.'
- 'People don't like me.'
- 'I'm not pretty.'

Write down the beliefs that took hold in those moments.

Step 4: Identify the Strategy You Took On

Once you made that belief about yourself, how did you start behaving?

What became your go-to strategy to compensate for that feeling of lack?

Did you start:

- Working harder than everyone else?
- Becoming the "good one" or the peacemaker?
- Always needing to win or be the best?
- Staying invisible to avoid rejection?
- Taking care of others so they wouldn't leave?

Write down the specific ways you adapted—the identity or behaviour you took on to stay safe, be accepted, or prove your worth.

Step 5: Get in Touch With the Feeling

For each strategy for success, ask yourself:

- How has living this way actually left me feeling, both when I succeeded and when I didn't?
- In the moment of success—or just after—what did you actually feel? Was it a true sense of fulfillment? If it was

there, how long did it last? Or did it fade quickly, leaving behind a familiar emptiness?

- What has it really felt like to always be pushing, proving, striving, or hiding?

Don't rush this. Slow down. Let yourself feel it.

This step is key to breaking the pattern and making space for something more real.

Step 6: Create a New Way of Being

Now ask: What would success look like if it came from your *true self*, not from fear or proving?

What new way of being could replace the old strategy?

For example:

- Replace *pushing to be the best* with *being grounded and present.*
- Replace *working to be loved* with *being generous and self-honouring.*

Write down who you're now committed to being. Then, write one or two small ways you can practice this in real life—today or this week.

> Over time, this new way of being will stop feeling like something you're trying to become and will start being who you naturally are.
>
> Keep catching yourself. Keep recommitting.
>
> Let go of who you thought you had to be… and become who you really are.

There's a lot going on here, if you feel you need any additional support, please head to www.willsteel.com/freetolead.

REFLECTION QUESTIONS

Reflect on your life and consider the decisions and beliefs that have shaped who you have become. By understanding these patterns, you can begin to shift your focus from simply producing results to finding true fulfillment. You can shift to some higher purpose that inspires you, rather than living your life to prove something, overcome something, or trying to 'win'.

Ask yourself:

1. How have these beliefs influenced my actions and behaviours?
2. What choices have I made based on the need to prove myself or compensate for perceived inadequacies?
3. How has this all impacted my life?

CHAPTER TAKEAWAYS:

» External results, while not invalid, are only fulfilling in the right context. If the context is making up for some lack in yourself, you won't be fulfilled. If the context is for some higher purpose, one that inspires you, the whole game is fulfilling, not just when you finally produce the results.

» When we are driven to produce results, we are often compensating for limiting beliefs and perceived inadequacy.

» Once we've identified our strategies for success, we can catch them at play, intervene, and choose to operate in alignment with our true selves, in fittra.

Chapter 10

CONQUERING SELF-SABOTAGE

'Self-sabotage is your brain's way of trying to keep you in familiar territory. Unless you are super self-aware, you are destined to repeat the same destructive patterns over and over.'

Does this sound familiar: You're just about to be successful, and you do something stupid or you forget to do something important, or mysteriously, you don't do something you know you need to do, and ultimately, you sabotage your success?

Self-sabotage can also manifest itself in subtle ways, such as procrastination, avoidance, or even making 'mistakes' at crucial times. Maybe you ask yourself questions like, 'Why do I always do this? Why do I always screw it up?' But when you learn to look beneath the surface and understand where these behaviours stem from, you get the chance to break your patterns of self-sabotage. So, if you want to be successful, and you keep falling at the last hurdle, then this chapter is especially for you. It's useful for all leaders to recognise not only their own self-sabotage patterns but also the patterns of the people who work for them.

SELF-SABOTAGE AND FEAR

Self-sabotage often arises from a fear of success or the responsibilities that come with it. Our limiting beliefs, often buried deep in our subconscious minds, can trigger fear and hesitation, preventing us from seizing new opportunities or embracing new challenges.

As discussed in Chapter 7, your brain, unbeknownst to you, is working in the background to protect you. It will have you do things unconsciously to avoid perceived danger. When you carry limiting beliefs, your brain can view success as a danger. Unfamiliar territory can feel threatening, prompting behaviours that bring you back to your comfort zone—even if that comfort zone includes struggle and underachievement. As a way of trying to protect you, your brain might act in irrational or impulsive ways, sabotaging success and keeping you in familiar, albeit unsatisfactory, territory. In the logic of the brain, it's better to fail now than *really* fail later. Remember, your brain's job is to help you survive. If you failed in the past, and you survived, even if it was upsetting or uncomfortable, when your brain perceives a threat, it will try to put you back there again and again. So, if you are interested in success, you first have to identify any self-sabotaging patterns that have been following you from your past.

SABOTAGING MY OWN SUCCESS

Until I discovered the tools you are learning in this book, I fell victim to self-sabotage many times, often during critical moments of my career. Once, I was given a huge new responsibility at work: to be responsible for all the local and regional seminar leaders in Europe. Being on time was a basic, non-breakable rule. I had an appointment scheduled with a senior coach who would be training me to take over the region. I literally got on the wrong train and showed up 45 minutes late. Instead of preparing diligently, I got caught up in minor, unrelated tasks, got distracted, and made what seemed like an innocent, stupid mistake. But it was not a mistake—it was my subconscious fear running the show.

I later realised that this was a pattern for me—a way of avoiding stepping into a new level of responsibility, accountability, and visibility. The fear wasn't about the position itself but about what it would mean to succeed. My perception was that if I succeeded, I would have even more to do than I currently had, and I would be held to account for producing more results. And even worse, I would be responsible for the results of others. I could see myself on endless hours of phone calls with leaders who were failing, using up every minute of my time. But there was something even deeper going on.

As a young child, I had seen my older brother being punished because he was the eldest and 'should be responsible'. I had it wired in me that the more responsible you are, the more severe the punishment would be if you made a mistake. Unbeknownst to me, my brain wasn't going to let that happen. And I just thought I'd gotten on the wrong train.

To overcome self-sabotage, it's essential to recognise the underlying fears and beliefs that drive these behaviours. Often, these fears are tied to childhood experiences or past failures that have shaped your perception. So, think about the most recent time you somehow sabotaged your own success, and take this opportunity to look at it for a moment. What was going on for you about the thing you were trying to be successful at? Did you really want it? Or was there fear about actually having that success? You could ask yourself, 'What was I afraid of? What would it have meant if I had been successful?'

SABOTAGING MY DREAM

I was just two flights away from graduating from the tactical weapons training school and becoming a fighter pilot. I remember sitting in the cockpit, thinking to myself, 'They think I'm good. But I'm barely hanging on by my fingernails here.' I knew if I moved on to the fast jet squadron and failed there, I'd be found out. Everyone would *really* know I wasn't that good. Guess what? On the very next trip, I had someone else draw my maps instead of doing them myself. They made an error, which caused me to fail at a crucial part of the trip. That was my last trip in a fast jet. It was over. I didn't go any further. I'd passed control over to someone else, subconsciously setting myself up for failure, and I didn't double check it thoroughly. Self-sabotage won the day.

If you want to be successful, it's critical to be clear about your self-sabotage mechanisms. I invite you to really self-reflect and identify the patterns, the thoughts you have, and how you feel about actually being successful. When you get closer and closer to success, you can be vigilant about your self-sabotage wanting to take over and ruin it for you.

This is why having a coach really supports people in breaking through these patterns and having success beyond what they've been able to accomplish—especially if it's in a new area. I've worked with thousands of entrepreneurs, and if we don't work to get their self-sabotage patterns identified, they will continue to struggle to produce the results they're committed to creating. No matter how sincere they are, no matter how much they say they want it, they will still sabotage their own success.

For example, one of my clients was running a business cleaning people's houses. She knew that if she wanted to grow the business, she had to employ more people, because she needed to focus her efforts on getting contracts and new customers. But time and time again, she found herself doing the cleaning herself, instead of trusting her employees to get the job done. Through our work together, we distinguished her underlying fear—that people would let her down. When she was a child, her father left home. She made his leaving mean that she couldn't trust people from that point forward. So now, as an adult, she lived with a fear of putting her trust in other people only to have them let her down. This made it hard for her to trust others to get the job done well—and this was causing her to sabotage the growth of her business. Once we got this fear distinguished and put a training and certification process in place for her new staff, we freed up her time to focus on growing her business, which she did. In fact, within 18 months, she grew it to 14 times the size it was when we started.

PROTECTING AGAINST SELF-SABOTAGE

When you can recognise your self-sabotage at play, you have the opportunity to intervene and not screw things up. Breaking away from self-sabotage takes real vigilance, and it often requires you to build structures of support to prevent you from slipping back into old patterns and making costly mistakes.

For example, early in my career, I found myself struggling with self-sabotage when I was leading introductory seminars to a program. I would often end late and then have insufficient time to support people working through their considerations about signing up for the program. Once I distinguished this behaviour as self-sabotage, I needed to put something in place to support me in staying on track. I implemented a practice of having my room manager hold up time signals for each section of the presentation, ensuring I had ample time at the end to take care of everyone. By doing this, I was able to consistently perform at a successful level.

In my journey, breaking free from self-sabotage required a willingness to confront uncomfortable truths about myself. I had to acknowledge my fears and doubts that were subtly directing my actions, and I had to acknowledge that, at times, I had been my own worst enemy.

The work you are doing in this book isn't easy. Confronting these truths about yourself can be uncomfortable. But that discomfort is nothing compared to living your life without fulfilling your dreams.

When you see self-sabotage surfacing, it's an opportunity to break old patterns and shatter old beliefs. The goal is to eliminate the constraints that are holding you back, allowing you to move forward without the weight of fear or self-doubt. When you feel stopped, fearful, or hesitant, you can use the exercises in this book to uncover the underlying causes. Ask yourself, 'Where is this coming from in my past? What does this remind me of? What did I decide at the time?' Then you can begin to understand how these beliefs have shaped your life, how they've made you feel, and how they've held you back from opportunities. Only then can you make a plan to keep from falling back into these habits. (Remember, it is very difficult to break out of self-sabotage alone. You will need to put in structures and practises to outsmart and trick your brain from taking over and sabotaging your success.)

EXERCISE: STOPPING SELF-SABOTAGE

Turn to a blank sheet of paper in your notebook and work through the following steps:

Step 1: Identify a Self-Sabotaging Moment

Think about a specific time when you made a 'mistake', procrastinated, or avoided preparing for something important, like a job interview or a test—and you failed.

Step 2: Dig Deeper

Now, it's time to take a deeper look into this moment. What were some of your fears and concerns? Were you afraid of failing? Afraid of succeeding? Was this a familiar pattern for you?

Step 3: Ask Yourself, 'What Was My Real Fear?'

Now that you've identified that you were afraid of success, or afraid of failure, etc., you can use the tool that should be becoming familiar to you by now—tracing those feelings back to the early moments where your limiting beliefs were formed. Ask yourself the following questions:

1. What does this remind me of? (See if you can identify a moment earlier in life when you had the same fear or feeling.)
2. What was happening?
3. Who was there?
4. What did it all mean?
5. What decisions did I make?
6. How is this now showing up in my current life? For example, 'That's making me afraid of XYZ.'

Step 4: Develop New Habits

Now, given that the fears you identified were made up and are now blocking your success, what could you put in place to make sure you don't sabotage your success moving forward? Is there a system or routine that can help keep you on track?

(Checklists, alarms, a schedule, or a new habit?)

Step 5: Seek Accountability

If you want more power to eliminate self-sabotage from your life, I recommend finding someone who can support you in avoiding those old patterns (a mentor, coach, colleague, friend, or anyone you trust to hold you accountable). Share what you've learned, create new support structures, and establish a system of accountability. For example, each week, make commitments to your coach about the actions you will take and those you will avoid. Your coach can hold you accountable for the promises you make and help you build powerful support systems. Over time, this process will retrain both you and your brain to operate beyond your self-sabotaging behaviours.

If you feel you need any additional support, please head to www.willsteel.com/freetolead.

REFLECTION QUESTIONS

1. When was a time I made a mistake at a crucial moment?
2. What patterns of self-sabotage have I fallen into in the past?
3. What underlying beliefs or fears were driving those self-sabotaging behaviours?

CHAPTER TAKEAWAYS

» Self-sabotage occurs when we subconsciously fear success or failure.

» The fears that lead to self-sabotage invariably stem from decisions made during earlier times in our lives when we experienced upset or failure in some way.

» Without the self-awareness to identify self-sabotaging behaviour, we are destined to repeat the same patterns over and over again, no matter how much we hate the results.

» If you can't dismantle your self-sabotaging behaviours on your own, get help.

A Bridge to Part 2

Before you move into Part 2, take a moment to reflect on the journey you've been on so far. You've confronted deep-seated limiting beliefs and learned how to shatter them. You've done the work to uncover your authentic self so you can stop living the way you think you're supposed to—and start living in fittra.

You've already begun doing incredible work.

Take a moment to acknowledge what you've already uncovered—it matters.

As you continue into Part 2, I want to remind you that transformation is a process. It often unfolds over months or even years, and usually with the support of a trained coach.

Even after doing the work, you may still find yourself slipping into old patterns, repeating automatic behaviours, or self-sabotaging. Your brain will try to pull you back into familiar territory—as we discussed in Part 1.

But now, you have something you didn't have before: awareness. The ability to recognise what's happening and step in. You can pause, reflect, and choose differently.

And when you find yourself stuck or repeating something you thought you'd let go of—go back. Revisit earlier chapters. Redo the exercises. That's not failure. That's the work.

This is how real change happens.

You've done a lot of work so far, but we're only halfway through the journey. From here, you get to decide how to use your newfound freedom. As you peel back the layers and break away from limiting beliefs and fears and the stories you've formed, you'll find that, in many ways, you're a blank slate. You have the space to create something new—something uniquely yours. Part 2 of this book is about stepping into your authentic leadership in fittra, free from the limiting beliefs of your past. We'll focus on how you can build on the freedom you've gained to lead with purpose and become a more effective (and likely less overworked) leader.

If you are feeling overwhelmed at this point in the journey or finding the work difficult, don't be discouraged. Consider working with a coach to help you work through the challenges you're facing and help you get greater results.

To learn more about me and my team, or if you feel you need any additional support, please head to www.willsteel.com/freetolead. Also, before we move on, you might like to watch the free video I mentioned earlier, where I coach people through dismantling the beliefs that once held them back. If you've already seen it, I recommend watching again—you'll often notice new things the second time. You can also find it at www.willsteel.com/freetolead.

PART 2

Creating Your Authentic Leadership

Chapter 11

REDEFINING LEADERSHIP

'A leader who tries to act the way they think they're supposed to will never be as effective as one who leads authentically.'

Picture the most controlling employer you have ever had. How did you feel around them? Were you motivated to do more? Inspired to stay and keep growing with the company? Or did you feel resentful about the work? It doesn't feel good to *be led* this way. And if we're being honest, most of us would agree that it doesn't feel good to *lead* this way either.

Traditional notions of leadership often emphasise authority, control, and a hierarchical approach to managing people and projects. But when you try to embody this type of leadership, you're not leading from your true self, in fittra. You're taking on an idea of leadership that doesn't start with you or what's important to you. Now, there may be times when you do need to micromanage people who are underperforming, such as someone who is not generating sufficient self-management or autonomy. Those are situations that have to be dealt with. As you develop your leadership and ability to empower the people you manage, these times should become less and less frequent.

What's important is to lead from within, not to try to show up the way you think a leader is 'supposed to' or to try to control a situation for the sake of appearing in control. (I will share an example of what this looks like in a moment.)

Consider that much of what you've believed about leadership might be what you've inherited, picked up, and even been told along the way. A leader who tries to act the way they think they're supposed to will never be as effective as one who leads authentically. Genuine leadership doesn't come from following a specific formula or behaving the way you think you should. It comes from showing up as who you really are and leading from there, authentically, in fittra.

When you learn to lead authentically, people around you know they can trust you. You are who you say that you are. You're committed to doing what you've said you're going to do, and you make decisions that move your business or your life towards a purpose. In this chapter, I'm going to show you why leading inauthentically won't get you the results you want, and how to start listening to, and leading from, your authentic self.

LEARNING TO LEAD AUTHENTICALLY

The first time I discovered the power of authentic leadership was when I went through my Royal Air Force Officer Training at RAF College Cranwell. My university friends, who had gone through the training before me, gave me what turned out to be bad advice. They said, 'Keep your head down, don't stand out. Just get through the training and hold your tongue.' So, I did.

After 16 weeks, my Flight Commander called me into his office and said, 'Steel, you're not officer material. You're like a ghost. Officers need to speak out and take command, so I can't recommend you for graduation. You have two choices— you can leave the Air Force, or we'll give you another shot and you can repeat the course.' I knew I wanted to be a pilot, and to be a pilot, I had to be an officer. So I elected the re-course.

When I got back to my room I slumped with my back against the door and started to cry. But that's when I had a moment of realisation. I told myself, 'Well that didn't work. I tried to be what I thought they wanted. But I wasn't being myself. This time I'm going to be myself and let whatever happens happen.' Just 18 weeks later, I graduated with the Leadership Trophy.

That wasn't the only time I found myself leading without authenticity. Sometimes in life we need to keep discovering the same lesson. In my second career, leading transformational programs, I found myself in a similar situation. I had finished my training and was almost at the end of my probationary period, and it was not looking good. I wasn't producing the results I needed to. I had one final course left to lead, which everything was riding on. But it was looking unlikely that I was going to pass.

To make matters worse, my final course seemed like an impossible task. I was set to lead a program in Van Nuys, a satellite location of the Los Angeles office of the company I was training with. The ultimate goal was to get participants from the course in Van Nuys to sign up for an advanced program in LA. Participants would have to navigate horrendous traffic delays, turning a 45-minute commute into a potential three-hour ordeal. Because of this, registrations into the senior course were notoriously low. No coach had managed to produce an acceptable result in over five years—and no one had *ever* achieved 42%, the conversion rate I needed in order to pass my probation.

The night before the course, I had a call with my coach, my mentor, and the performance team chairman. They were at a loss for what to coach me on. Everything they'd suggested thus far, and everything I'd tried, hadn't worked. The chairman said, 'Well, we don't have any coaching for you, given you're just gonna do whatever you do, regardless of whatever we say. So… *good luck*. We'll see if you're still a leader at the end of this course.' With that they hung up.

I was on my own. This was my crucible moment. I looked at myself in the mirror and said, 'Well, I've tried everything I know. I've tried to lead like I think I'm supposed to lead and it hasn't worked. I'm just going to go out there and really love these people—and let the chips fall where they may.'

So, I let go of everything I thought I was 'supposed to do.' Instead, I simply spoke from the heart, as my true self. I shared my stories and insights. I encouraged the participants to explore their own lives and dig deep into their past. But I also listened to my intuition. I paid attention to my authentic self, I listened to my gut, and I spoke up when I needed to. Throughout the course, I challenged and pushed the participants where they needed it. I led with real authenticity.

The course was a success. Over 50% of the participants

registered into the advanced program. The attendees even brought hundreds of guests to their final session because they wanted everyone they knew to do this program. I'll share more later in this chapter about what I did that made such a difference, but for now the lesson is this: **The most powerful leader you can be is *being* your *authentic* self.**

That's why Part 1 of this book is the foundation. You need to shatter your limiting beliefs and transform into your true self before you can lead authentically. Being able to then lead from your true self, regardless of your environment and external pressures, takes something extra. It takes *courage*. That courage comes from creating, practising, developing, and empowering your authentic leadership, which is what you'll learn in Part 2.

It's also why you're not going to find scripts or a guide on what *to do* as a leader in this book. Instead, you're going to learn how to focus on *who you are being* as a leader. My strapline for coaching business owners and leaders is, **Transform the Leader, Transform the Business.** This is *the key*. So the real questions to keep asking yourself are, **'Who am I being right now?'** and **'Who am I committed to being?'** Anytime the answers to those questions don't align, you aren't leading authentically, and that means you need to adjust.

IDENTIFYING THE INAUTHENTIC SELF

The precursor to leading authentically is recognising and telling the truth about when you are *not* being your authentic self.

Some signs to look out for include:

- Leading like you were told you should lead.
- Leading like you've seen and experienced other people lead, thinking that is how you're supposed to lead.
- Leading with force to avoid being seen as weak.
- Getting frustrated with your team.
- Not saying what you truly want to say out of fear of upsetting people, or a concern for what they might think or say about you.
- Avoiding or ignoring situations.
- Putting off doing what you know and planned to do.
- Cutting corners or not doing things the way they're meant to be done or designed to be done.
- Not doing things to the best of your ability.
- Not demanding of others to perform to the best of their abilities.
- Not delegating because of your fear that things won't get done, or telling yourself it's easier to just do it yourself.
- Not taking the time to ensure that people are clear about what you've asked them to do.
- Not keeping your promises or holding others to account for the promises they've made.
- Walking over things, ignoring things, or pretending everything's 'okay' when it isn't.
- Not going the extra mile when it's required.
- Not addressing issues to your satisfaction and then feeling resentful.
- Feeling underpowered, constrained, or repressed.

If you find yourself falling into any of these modes, stop, tell the truth, and recognise that you are not being true to your authentic self. Then ask yourself, **'What am I committed** to here?' This will interrupt the automatic behaviour that is running the show and give you space to turn your leadership around on a dime.

At first, this might feel difficult. You will almost certainly need to generate courage to interrupt the status quo so you can start showing up authentically. But the more you practise identifying where you are not showing up as your true self, and the more you speak from your authentic voice, the easier it will be to lead *being* the true you.

SPEAKING AND LEADING AUTHENTICALLY

Once you start identifying when you aren't leading from your true self, and correcting that, the next piece is to start *listening* to the real you. As we identified in Chapter 5, the real you is limitless. We all have a natural leader within us—a leader who knows what we want, what we are committed to, what we need to do, and what we need to say. But we talk ourselves out of listening to that self. We worry about what others might think, or we put off situations that need our attention.

But if we listen to our authentic selves and do what needs to be done or say what needs to be said, there's real power there.

For example, in the middle of leading the aforementioned program in Van Nuys, I had started to get the sense that these people were all enjoying the course—but *real transformation* was not happening. I knew that I needed to say or do something different. After all, I had committed to showing up as myself and loving the participants no matter what.

On the second day, I was preparing to send the participants on their meal break. I had given them an assignment to accomplish over this break—to reach out to the people in their lives that they hadn't been communicating with, that they needed to talk to, and have the conversations they needed to have with those people. I asked the group, 'How many of you are taking on the assignment this break?' Only a few hands went up, so I asked, 'Well, what are you going to be doing on the break?' Some of them called out jokingly, 'Eating!'

So I told them, 'Okay, we're not going on a break then. You guys are not taking your transformation seriously.' I asked them why they were even here taking the course in the first place. Some people responded, saying things like 'to transform my relationships' 'deal with my life' or 'to be happy'.

I said, 'Well, talking to the other people here during the break isn't going to transform your life. Who would you need to be speaking to if you wanted to transform the relationships and situations in your life?'

They finally acknowledged that if they wanted true transformation, they would need to be having conversations with the people in their lives with whom they have issues.

So I said, 'Okay, either have those conversations with the people in your life, or don't bother coming back after the break. You're wasting your time and mine. Stop being a passive observer in your life and start to be someone who actually *deals* with your life, where and when it's happening, which is always right now, not later.'

I asked again for a show of hands from those who were actually going to have the conversations they needed to have during the break.

This time, almost every hand went up.

When I went on my break, I was suddenly gripped with

fear. What if I had pushed them too hard? I imagined half of the people not coming back. I wondered if I had just trashed the course, setting myself up to get fired. So, what did I do? Instead of giving into this fear, I recommitted. I went to my room, looked at myself in the mirror and told myself, 'You promised to love these people, no matter what. You were committed to helping them transform their lives. Be your word, not your feelings. Cause a transformation in every interaction.'

When we resumed from the meal break, every single participant came back. I asked who wanted to share a breakthrough they had had on the break, and almost every hand in the room went up. What they shared was amazing. People had reached out and gotten in touch with parents they hadn't spoken to in decades. They connected, forgave past actions, and asked for forgiveness for not getting in touch sooner and for holding on to their resentments.

This was the power of transformation in action. But, if I had not listened to my authentic self and had ignored what I *knew* I needed to tell them, they would have come back from the break the same people who left. Instead, they came back having altered their lives forever. What if I hadn't acted when I knew that I needed to? What if I hadn't listened to myself? What if I had instead listened to the voice of doubt, trying to talk me out of saying something? That massive transformation for all those participants would not have happened.

When you don't listen to your authentic self, or when you overlook things out of fear of upsetting people or worrying what others might think, you're letting your own limiting beliefs get in the way of making a difference for those around you. Listening to your true self. Leading from there, does take practice. But it becomes easier every time. The more you lean into your true self, the more power you will have as an authentic leader, and the more you will grow as a human being. **Your leadership will grow as you grow.**

EXERCISE: PRACTISING AUTHENTIC LEADERSHIP

In this chapter, we've looked at what it means to lead authentically and the power that comes when you are genuinely being yourself in the face of challenges. Let's take these insights and put them into practice.

On a blank page in your notebook, work through these steps:

1. Reflect on a Recent Leadership Moment
Think about a recent experience where you were leading, guiding a project, or working with others to solve a problem. Look back on how you were showing up. Were you leading as your true self, or were you putting on an act, holding back, and avoiding speaking up and saying what needed to be said? Simply said, was there something to say that you didn't say? Or was there something to do that you didn't do?

2. Identify What You Were Afraid of
What fears, doubts, or concerns cropped up for you during that time? Were you worried about how people might see you? Were you avoiding conflict? Did you doubt yourself, second guess your choices, or feel hesitant?

3. Imagine Leading from Your True Self
Picture how you would approach that situation if you were

leading from your most authentic self, fully aligned with what you care about and are committed to (the real you we unlocked in Chapter 5). What would be different? Write down the changes you would make in what you would have said, the actions you would have taken, and in your overall approach.

4. Make a Commitment to Authenticity

Pick one area of your life—whether it's work, personal relationships, or a particular project—where you'll commit to showing up as your true self. What would this look like in reality? Identify three specific steps you could take to start showing up authentically in this area right away.

Possible examples:

- You could tell the truth about something you've been tolerating that's not okay for you.
- You could apologise for something you did or said that you know was coming from a place of frustration.
- You could offer to pay for any damage you've done or ask how you could make it up to the person.
- You could have a conversation with someone you felt distant from with the commitment to resolve whatever is causing that distance.
- You could get back to people that you know are waiting for you to respond and acknowledge that you avoided getting back to them.
- You could acknowledge someone for the great work they've done.
- You could appreciate someone for something they did for you.

- You could pay back money you owe and have been avoiding paying back.
- Etc.

5. *Daily Reflection*

Over the next few weeks, carve out a few minutes each day to check in on how you're doing. What feels different? Are you noticing more ease or confidence in your leadership? At the end of each day, write down three ways you made progress that day. At the start of the next day, take a moment to read back through what you wrote the day before.

You could also rate yourself each day on a scale of 0 – 10 based on how authentically you led, with 0 being not at all and 10 being 100 percent. Then, reflect on ways you can improve. Doing this daily will fuel your commitment to leading from your true self, in fittra.

REFLECTION QUESTIONS

1. Have I been leading authentically, or am I leading some way I *think* I'm supposed to?
2. Do I question myself or wonder what others would do in this situation?
3. What kind of leader am I committed to being?

CHAPTER TAKEAWAYS

» Being an authentic leader isn't about exercising control. It's about listening to our true selves and leading from there.

» When we can identify where we're *not* showing up authentically, it becomes easier to speak as our authentic selves.

» Authentic leaders don't have to worry about scripts or specific ways of acting. They lead from what they're authentically committed to and what really matters to them, and they speak up.

Chapter 12

CREATING A VISION
THAT INSPIRES

*'A vision is more than just a set of goals or targets—
it's a powerful image of the future that you are
passionate about creating.'*

In the last chapter, I asked you to picture the worst employer you've had. Now, I'd like you to ask you a different question. Which employer, teacher, or leader in your life had the biggest positive impact on you? What was it about them that stood out?

It likely wasn't that they micromanaged or controlled everything. I'm guessing that the reason has more to do with their ability to inspire or motivate you.

Authentic leaders are able to inspire others, and they do this by having a vision. A vision is more than a set of goals or targets; it's a powerful image of the future that you are passionate about creating. A clear, authentic vision acts as a magnet, aligning the strengths of your team towards a shared aim.

So how do you create that kind of vision? It starts with asking yourself, **'What's my purpose in life?'**

PURPOSE VS. VISION

Your purpose should be expressed in you doing something you love to do and want to do. The vision is the dream. The purpose is the reason for doing what you're doing in the first place. For example, my purpose in life is to make a difference. My vision is to ultimately work with world leaders and help them make decisions that impact the lives of millions of people. So you can start with your purpose in life, and then ask yourself, 'What's the fullest expression? What's the biggest possible vision of that purpose being realised in the world?'

An authentic vision aligns with your true self and the broader good, creating a deeper meaning for what you are doing.

My work in developing leadership programs in the Middle East was initially a way for me to fulfil my purpose in life. I knew I could make a difference by empowering individuals to lead from their true authentic selves, in fittra. This was not just about professional development but also about fostering a cultural shift towards greater self-expression and authenticity. For example, many of the women I spoke to in the Middle East experienced being constrained in a male-dominated environment. They found it difficult to assert themselves, and they worried about what others would think of them. This kept them from speaking up and offering their best ideas out of fear of others stealing those ideas and getting all the credit. This is one of many examples I heard of women holding themselves back. I often heard the phrase, 'It's just the way it is.'

The more women I spoke to, the more I saw that they didn't realise that phrase, was actually them being resigned to the idea that nothing else was possible. In fact, I spoke to one woman who was a senior manager in the oil and petroleum industry in Saudi Arabia who worked really long hours but suffered from extreme anxiety around having interactions with colleagues and team members at her work. After many stories like this, I got inspired to empower these women to lead as their authentic selves, with their true natural feminine energy, contributing their strengths and ideas to their companies and organisations. What if they were free to contribute with their innate nurturing and empathetic nature?

The men that I worked with in that environment had their own stories often centered on not making mistakes, not being seen as weak, and not challenging authority. They felt afraid to be themselves, or to communicate when they had problems. I wanted to empower them to discover their true selves, their true essence, and be emboldened to create their own unique authentic leadership from there.

So, the work began to take shape, all inside my purpose, to make a difference. And as we led more and more programs, this purpose opened up a much larger vision: **Transforming the Leadership of the Middle East.** This not only inspired me but also my team and the participants. If you ask anyone in my team what we're up to or why we're doing what we're doing, they'll tell you, we're 'Transforming the leadership of the Middle East.' (I will walk you through the steps I took to end up with this vision shortly.)

Perhaps this vision sounds too big or too bold to you. Or who am I, some English guy, to go transform the leadership of the Middle East? But the better question is, who am I not to be?

The point is, whatever you're doing, challenge yourself to think beyond the obvious. Go beyond simply accomplishing a task or doing something because you said you would or were told to. Ask yourself, what's the fullest, most impactful expression of what I'm doing? How could what I'm doing make the biggest difference in the world?

OPPORTUNITY TO PRACTISE: CREATING A VISION

The first step in creating your vision is to get clear about your purpose. A simple way to do this is to look at what you have in front of you, whether you're working on business goals, or doing some mundane task that simply needs to be done, etc., and ask yourself, 'Why am I doing this? Why do I care about this? What's my life about that has me doing this?' Answer by stating and completing the following phrase:

'This matters to me because my life is about

_____.'

With whatever answer you come up with, see if you can make it even more powerful. To do this, ask yourself:

'And why do I care about *that*? Why does *that* matter to me?'

Again, answer by completing the phrase:

'*This* matters to me because my life is about

_____.'

Keep repeating this questioning process until your answer is inspiring to you and feels true to who you are. It's not about trying to figure it out—in fact, *don't* figure it out. Just start the phrase and keep speaking, and see what comes out of your mouth. When what comes out of your mouth inspires you and moves you, then that's your purpose.

Now, in the middle of your day, you might not be conscious of your purpose. It's easy to lose sight of your *why* as life throws its challenges at you. But if you do the work above to get clear about your purpose, then when you're not present to it, or struggling, you can ask yourself, 'Okay, why am I doing this? What's my purpose here?' (I'll talk more about using your purpose to make business decisions in Chapter 15.)

Now you have your purpose, you can go about creating your vision. To create your vision, ask yourself:

'If I were to truly fulfil my purpose, what's the greatest impact it could have in the world? What's the ultimate, most inspiring outcome I could accomplish?'

Keep asking yourself this question until your answer is inspiring and moving to you.

In my example, I asked myself, 'Why am I leading programs in the Middle East?' The first answer was, 'Because Ahmed invited me to.' The next answer was, 'It's an opportunity to fulfill my purpose—to make a difference and empower others to do the same.' Ultimately, I realised that if enough people were empowered to make a difference, we could address the world's biggest challenges (communities and nations working together to end poverty, hunger, war, and more). I arrived at this statement, 'What we are up to is transforming the leadership of the Middle East.' And that became my vision.

To reiterate, first get clear about your purpose—why you do what you do—and from there, create a vision. Ultimately, you're answering the question, **'What's the biggest, most inspiring context I can create for my life with what I'm doing?'** It's not fanciful or trite. It's not just making something up that sounds nice. It needs to be connected to what really matters to you. The bolder and more audacious the vision, the more power and creativity it will give you and your team in dealing with what you're experiencing in the present moment.

This doesn't just apply to business. Let's say you don't run a company or have a leadership position— you're a stay-at-home parent. You can ask yourself in the middle of a tantrum, 'What am I doing here? Why am I doing this?'

You might say, 'I want my kids to behave well.' 'I don't want my kids to be spoiled and entitled.'

Then you could ask, 'Why do I care about *that*?' 'I want my kids to be strong, independent, and live great lives.'

'Why do I care about that?' 'I want my kids to be happy and fulfilled in life. I want my kids to grow up and be their fullest expression in the world.' Great—now you have your purpose. From here, what's the biggest, boldest, most audacious expression of that in the world? Maybe your vision is, 'My kids grow up to be healthy, wholesome human beings who create a great life for themselves and their children.' That's a vision.

WORKING TOWARDS A VISION

Having a clear vision doesn't only inspire you—it keeps you going when things get tough (and helps others around you do the same). Even the most well-oiled machine, the best organised team, will face difficult challenges together. So, what is it that keeps some teams pushing through tough times, while others become disconnected and disgruntled? Or, in some cases, even give up? Those that give up usually are not operating inside a clear, vibrant vision. Those that keep going do so because they're inspired to realise their vision. An alive and present vision is what will help people to keep going through challenges—to go the extra mile to solve problems while bringing forth their creativity. Fewer people will leave the team when they're working towards, inspired by, and connected to a great vision.

In my work in the Middle East, for example, we faced one particular hurdle. There was some resistance for potential customers to commit to our four-day program, flying in from other countries and paying the price we needed to charge to maintain profitability. We had to decide what to do. If we lowered our price, we wouldn't be able to sustain the program. But we were committed to transforming the leadership of the Middle East, so we stood in that vision and looked from there to see what we could change. By centering on our vision, we came up with a smaller, easier first step, creating a shorter two-day program that would be available not only in person, but also online at a more palatable price.

We forged ahead inside our vision and ended up scheduling the course in Casablanca, Morocco. Around 40 participants attended in person in the event room, and 80 participants attended online via Zoom. There were a lot of details to sort out. I needed to lead in English, while being simultaneously translated into Arabic through headsets for the participants, and then have what the participants were saying be interpreted into English for me through my headset. We also needed to fully include the people on Zoom with the people in the room so all attendees could experience truly being part of the same event.

This was a huge challenge. It seemed like issues were popping up right and left, including internet interruptions, interpreters struggling to understand participants speaking in a Moroccan dialect, needing to really listen to hear if the participants were actually getting what I was saying versus the often incorrect translation of the interpreters. There were moments when it started to feel impossible. At one point, I was wearing a headset listening to a participant speaking in Arabic, a translator speaking to me in English, my partner correcting the translator in Arabic, and my own voice, all being amplified through the same headset. Can you imagine having to coach somebody with all that going on?

I had to constantly remind myself that this was what transforming the leadership of the Middle East looked like at this moment. When we encountered issues, recentering on the vision gave me focus to resolve problems and have the patience to take the time to really understand the participants, while keeping things moving forwards. I consciously kept refocusing on the difference we were committed to making whenever things got difficult. And I would remind myself, my team, and the participants of our commitment. **Having a clear vision keeps you centered, grounded, and focused.**

WHO DO YOU NEED TO BE TO REALISE THE VISION?

One of the most powerful questions you can ask yourself when you're working towards a larger purpose is, 'Who do

I need to be right now?' Not only for the big challenges but also for addressing and handling the more mundane details.

When my team and I were handling the situation in Casablanca, I constantly asked myself who I needed to be in those moments. The answer wasn't always the same. Sometimes I needed to be patient and encouraging. Sometimes I needed to take command and steer the ship. And I always needed to be grateful and connected to the participants and team while leading the program. (This doesn't mean abandoning who you are. The answer to 'Who do I need to be right now?' should always come from the authentic you. But you might have to lead differently in different moments. Listening to your authentic self will help you know what to say, how to show up, and what to do.)

When you answer the question, 'Who do I need to be right now?' and show up as that person, you will inspire your team, keeping them connected to both the immediate tasks at hand and the bigger picture.

EXERCISE: CREATING YOUR VISION

On a blank sheet of paper in your notebook, work through these steps to create your vision:

1. Think Big

Focus on one area where you are a leader, or where you want to be a leader. This might be within your family, within your business or your workplace, or within your community.

Answer these questions to start to create your big vision:

- What is it that I really want? What's my dream? (And, if you don't have a dream, what could it be?)

- What change do I want to see in the world, my industry, or my community?
- Why is this important to me, why do I care? (Remember to keep repeating this until your answer is moving and inspiring for you.)

2. Start With an Overview Plan
What would need to happen for your big vision to be realised? Just say what needs to happen. Don't get bogged down in details on how to do it.

3. Create a 12-Month Plan
What needs to happen over the next 12 months? Again, don't get too bogged down in the details.

4. Create a 6-Month Plan
What needs to happen in the next 6 months to be on track to realise your 12-month plan?

5. Create a 3-Month Plan
What needs to happen in the next 3 months to be on track for your 6-month plan?

6. Create a 1-Month Plan
Now you can get more specific. What actions need to happen in this coming month to be on track for your 3-month plan?

7. Plan Your Actions for the Coming Week
List what actions you can take this week to be on track for accomplishing what you need to accomplish this first month.

8. Schedule a Weekly Progress Check-In
Schedule a weekly time to review the actions you took and the results you produced in the past week. Then, revise and

create new actions for the upcoming week, keeping in mind that your 3-month, 6-month, and 12-month goals are getting closer. Check if any adjustments are needed, and try not to get discouraged if you find them. You may not realise this, but airplanes are off course about 90% of the time on long-haul flights. I know, I used to be a pilot.

9. Decide Who You Need to Be

For each step, ask yourself, 'Who do I need to be to make this happen?' (Make sure you're creating this from your authentic self while staying committed to your vision.) Write your answer down and commit to being that way. As challenges and obstacles come up, remember to keep asking yourself, 'Who do I need to be here?' You will need to show up as this for yourself, your team, your family, or whoever you're leading.

If you feel you need any additional support, please head to www.willsteel.com/freetolead.

REFLECTION QUESTIONS

1. If I could create a big change in my world or the world at large, what would it be?
2. What would need to happen for this to be realised?
3. Who would I need to be to have this happen?

CHAPTER TAKEAWAYS

» A clear expansive vision built on your purpose inspires not only you but the people around you to be motivated and committed

» Working in line with your purpose and inside of fulfilling your vision helps you and others overcome challenges and keep moving forward.

» You might need to show up as a different *you* in different situations (this doesn't mean abandoning your true self, but showing up as the version of your authentic self that can inspire and encourage others in that moment).

Chapter 13

THE POWER OF
EMPOWERING OTHERS

'How you listen to people determines how big they will become. If you listen to them as small, weak, less intelligent, or incapable, then that's how they will show up.'

For many of us, the traditional top-down, hierarchal approach of leadership is deeply ingrained. But if we think about leaders who we gravitate towards, it becomes clear that those leaders have something special. And I'm not just talking about charisma. The most effective leaders make others feel seen, heard, and understood. This compels people to *want* to perform and contribute.

Great leaders empower their teams to excel. They delegate responsibility, they have the courage to trust their people to make decisions, and they embolden them with a sense of autonomy.

Firstly, note that I said delegating *responsibility*, not just delegating tasks. Delegating tasks is in the domain of *doing*. Delegating responsibility is in the domain of *being*. If it's clear that you are responsible for the outcome of what you're doing, you will naturally take more ownership. This creates a sense of power and autonomy and an expanded sense of self. Imagine if all the people you led felt that way and acted that way about what you're trying to accomplish together. How would that transform your results?

When you lead with trust, you create an environment where people feel confident to take initiative and contribute their best ideas. When people feel empowered, they are more engaged, innovative, and persistent—they're willing to go the extra mile.

In 1997, I attended a leadership program hosted by the organisation I was working for. I noted that one of the participants, who I'll call Orlaith, was from Ireland. This caught my attention because my grandfather was Irish. That's when an idea formed. I thought, '*What if we took this program to Ireland?*' On one of the breaks I made a point of speaking to Orlaith. I said to her, 'Hey, Orlaith. I've thought about taking the program to Ireland.' She immediately responded with, 'I'm with ya!'

The next thing I knew, she was on the stage announcing to everyone, 'Will and I are taking the program to Ireland!' This felt like more pressure than I had bargained for. I sank down in my seat. What had I started?

However, the next morning when I awoke, I was so inspired by the idea that I was moved to tears. What transpired over the next two years was Orlaith and I partnering up. I personally trained her to lead introductions to the program in people's homes. Before we knew it, Orlaith was leading two or three introductions a week in remote areas of Ireland, with people who would have never had access to this type of event otherwise. She once drove over four hours from Sligo to Cork to lead an event. Only one person showed up, and they didn't sign up. Disappointed, Orlaith drove the four hours home, with a painful bad back, convinced she was a failure and no good.

I spent the next morning, and many other mornings, getting her head sorted out, reminding her of her courage and commitment: her dream to have transformation available for the people in Ireland. Over time, she began to have people register, and eventually other Irish people became motivated and inspired with Orlaith's vision. In turn, they got themselves trained to lead introductions. Finally, we got permission to schedule a program in Dublin. We filled it with around a hundred people, and it became a huge success. People came from all over Ireland to attend the final session on the Tuesday evening to find out about this program their family member or friend had been attending that preceding weekend. That was back in the year 2000. Since that first program, more than 6,000 people have completed the program in Ireland.

What would have happened if I had never put my trust in Orlaith? If I hadn't shared my vision with her? Or if I hadn't trusted her to be the one to take it on? If I had chosen to replace her instead of encouraging her when she repeatedly failed? We wouldn't have the impact we created. But through empowering Orlaith, through giving her the opportunity to step up and be a leader, 6,000 people's lives were transformed.

WHAT DOES IT MEAN TO EMPOWER OTHERS?

So you might be thinking, 'Well, *how* do I empower my team? How do I empower the people around me to step up and be leaders?' **Empowering others requires listening actively, valuing diverse perspectives, and recognising the unique strengths of each of your team members.**

Listening Actively

Let me share with you one of my experiences of being empowered to become a leader. In 1997, I attended and participated in a transformational program. I was impressed and in awe of the person leading. He was direct, bold, and when he interacted with people, oftentimes what he said was startling. His interrogative questioning of participants left me in disbelief. I couldn't believe he had the audacity, clarity, and foresight to say what he was saying, and say it without any edge or malice. His words seemed to cut through all the unconscious fluff around what people were saying. People were shocked to discover that someone could perceive what was really going on with them, things that in many cases they were not even aware of themselves. I had the thought, *'I wish I could be like that. That guy is unbelievable.'*

This program included a follow-up seminar series, which we attended weekly to reinforce and practice what we had learned. Just before one of these weekly sessions, I was chatting with the seminar leader, who I'll call JD, in the foyer outside the main room. I said, 'I think I'd like to be a program leader.' His eyes grew, and I experienced he was really listening and taking me seriously. It was as if his ears grew really big. His response was, 'Yeah, I get it. I think you'd be a really great one.'

I reeled back. I felt seen, understood, and validated. He really *got* me. Someone believed in me. At that moment, I knew it was possible. I knew I could do it. And now it was all I wanted to do.

What if you could be *that person* for the people you lead, like JD was for me? The one person who believed in me? The one person who heard me, got me, and saw me as bigger than I saw myself? The point is, how you listen to people determines how big they will become. If you listen to them as small, weak, less intelligent, or incapable, then that's how they will show up.

If you want the best from your people, you must actively listen. It's not just about hearing them, but about choosing to listen and trusting that they are capable of achieving bigger and better things. This will require you to consciously create your perception in the face of whatever automatic thoughts you may have about the person. But if you speak and act from there, you'll be amazed how people will respond to you. After all, how often do people feel acknowledged, appreciated, and valued for who they are and what they contribute? Not often enough.

Valuing Diverse Perspectives

Great leaders encourage the people they lead to share their perspectives and contribute ideas. This doesn't mean you have to then change what you're doing or do it their way. But rather than railroading them into doing what you want them to do, it's much more empowering if you validate their view. And sometimes they'll have an idea that you hadn't thought of or they'll highlight something you weren't aware of. At the very least, they'll appreciate being heard, having an input, and feeling that you consider their view. It's much like being a parent. You can either say, 'This is the way it is. We're doing it this way,' or you can validate their viewpoint, listen to them, and then make the ultimate decision.

If the people you lead feel that what they have to say is not important, and that they just have to do whatever it is that you say, they won't feel empowered to share ideas or contribute. And even worse, they're unlikely to take ownership. If they feel part of the decision-making process, then the decision feels like something you've made together. Instead of just *doing* the task, they experience *being* part of the team.

Recognising the Strengths of Your Team Members – Let Them Shine

One way to really empower your team is to recognise what each of them is good at. This may sound obvious, but just because somebody is not good at one particular task doesn't mean they can't be great at another. When proposing a plan, you could even ask your team, 'Who wants to be responsible for XYZ?' This allows people to step up and excel at what they do best.

Also, consider this approach when you're wondering how to accomplish something. Rather than asking yourself, 'How do I do this?' Ask yourself, 'Who can I get to do this? Who on my team could figure this out?' By taking this simple approach, you will unburden yourself from having to figure everything out on your own. Stop trying to figure out everything yourself, and ask your team—that's what they're there for.

Who doesn't want to be asked for help with something they're great at, or be challenged to figure something out, and be a hero? Human beings like to help. They like to solve problems. They like to feel useful. And they love to be recognised, valued, acknowledged, and appreciated for what they contribute.

RECOMMENDED PRACTISE

- Go out of your way to actively practise listening to people while thinking of them as big and capable. Recognise which negative, automatic thoughts come in, and don't listen to them. Say, 'No, no, no. This person is great.' Speak, listen, and act from there.
- Practise asking people for their views and ideas before you give them the final solution.
- Practise interrupting your thoughts when you try to figure out how to do everything, and instead reach out to your team and ask for support.

REFLECTION QUESTIONS

1. Am I empowering my team to take ownership, or am I suppressing them?
2. Am I listening to my team as big and capable or am I listening to them as small and incompetent?
3. Am I surrounding myself with people who are more capable than me in their specialty?

CHAPTER TAKEAWAYS

» True leadership is about empowering others and emboldening them to take on challenges.

» How we think about people when we listen to them is how they show up.

» To delegate powerfully is to delegate responsibility, not just assign tasks.

» You don't have to figure out everything yourself. People love to shine.

Chapter 14

OPERATING WITH INTEGRITY

'Every time you choose integrity in small moments, you build the strength to tackle the bigger ones with confidence and ease.'

If I had to boil authentic leadership down to one core principle, it would be integrity. Integrity is the foundation on which true leadership is built. After all, if you're not being your true self, how could you possibly feel whole and complete? When you act in ways that aren't aligned with who you really are, a sense of disconnection or fragmentation sets in. That's not morality—that's simply misalignment.

We all recognise the term integrity, and most people agree it's important. But what it actually means can vary widely.

The Cambridge dictionary defines integrity as the quality of being honest and committed to your moral principles, or being complete, and whole.[1] Merriam Webster defines it

1 *Meaning of Integrity in English - Cambridge Dictionary*, dictionary.cambridge.org/us/dictionary/english/integrity. Accessed 19 Feb. 2025.

as firmly standing in a moral code, being unimpaired and sound, or being complete and undivided.[2]

In the context of leadership, we're setting morality aside—not because ethics don't matter, but because morality is subjective and shaped by time and culture. Instead, we're focusing on integrity as a source of power, alignment, and effectiveness.

The way we're defining integrity here can be separated into three parts, but the three parts work together to form a whole:

- Honouring your word
- Being your authentic self
- Functioning consistently with your vision

Taken together, these make up a practical foundation for leading with integrity.

With regard to leadership, what matters is that you *function* with integrity. It's not like integrity is a quality you either have or you don't. Rather, integrity is something to take on.

HONOURING YOUR WORD

It's my belief that one of the most powerful things you can develop as an authentic leader is the strength of your word. When you keep your promises—to others **and to yourself**—you build a deep internal trust. You begin to relate to yourself as someone who follows through, who can be relied upon. That's not just empowering; it's profoundly transformative.

Because the truth is, **how you relate to your own word**

---

2 "Integrity Definition & Meaning." *Merriam-Webster*, Merriam-Webster, www.merriam-webster.com/dictionary/integrity. Accessed 19 Feb. 2025.

shapes how you show up in the world. When I give my word to another, I'm also giving my word to myself that I will keep that promise. And when I honour that, even in the smallest moments, I grow in confidence, clarity, and power. But when I don't, something inside me shrinks. I lose trust in myself. That erosion may be subtle at first, but over time it weakens leadership at its core.

When you stop brushing aside the promises you make to yourself—to get fit, to stop avoiding, to follow through—and you start honouring them, something shifts. Your self-respect grows. Your sense of power grows. And from there, your leadership naturally expands.

And when you keep your word to others, especially when it's inconvenient or costs you personally, you become someone who people can truly rely on. That builds trust, credibility, and real influence. When you say you'll do something, they know you mean it and that you'll follow through. That kind of consistency is rare, and people notice. If you want to lead powerfully, it's not enough to sound good; you have to live what you say. That's what earns real respect: being someone who walks their talk.

BEING YOUR AUTHENTIC SELF

When you're true to who you are, there's nothing to manage, explain, or prove. You operate from a place of clarity and wholeness. But when you act in ways that don't align with your real self—when you put on a front, say what you think others want to hear, or compromise on your truth—you disconnect from yourself. You lose energy. You lose trust. You lose power. People around you will pick up on this. They might not say anything, or even be cognisant of what they're feeling, but your words and actions won't ring true for them. No amount of convincing or explaining or reasoning will motivate or influence them like it would if you were being true to your authentic self.

If you find yourself doubting or questioning yourself, or even getting angry, then this is an indication to you that you're not being true to your authentic self. When you are being true to your authentic self, and acting and speaking from there, you experience being grounded and solid—there is clarity. Your words, actions, and *being* are all one.

FUNCTIONING CONSISTENTLY WITH YOUR VISION

When you have a vision, and you keep that vision alive through time, it provides a source of inspiration and creativity, guiding the actions you take. This may be in the approach you adopt, what you say, what you tolerate, what you don't tolerate, and what you stand for. When you hit a challenge, or have a question about which path to take in your business and life, ask yourself, 'What decision will bring me closer to realising my vision? (We'll expand more on the process of using your purpose and vision for decision-making in the next chapter.)

This keeps you aligned with your authentic self, helping you maintain integrity and be true to who you are. Only through this process of standing in the vision, creating from the vision, and acting consistent with your vision, will you have any chance of actually *realising* the vision.

THE POWER OF INTEGRITY IN ACTION

What does it actually look like to lead with integrity? Integrity in action requires being honest, being true to your word, showing up as who you really are, being consistent, and firmly adhering to your values through time. Well, let me give you an example of someone who personified this in history. That leader is Mahatma Gandhi.

Few leaders embody the power of integrity quite like Gandhi did. For 32 years, he led India's fight for independence through nonviolent resistance (his vision). During that period, British authorities tested his resolve, and time after time, Gandhi stood firm in his truth (his authentic self). He refused to employ violence, no matter how difficult the circumstances became, because it violated his principles (he functioned consistently with his vision). His unwavering commitment ultimately led to India gaining independence.[3] That's the kind of impact integrity can have. It outlasts opposition, breaks through resistance, and creates real change.

But Gandhi's integrity wasn't just about his fight against British rule. After independence, India faced chaos as Hindus and Muslims turned against each other in violent clashes. Gandhi, heartbroken by the violence, once again stood by his word, embodying integrity. He took action. He began a fast, declaring he would not eat until the communities reconciled. Gandhi's integrity held so much weight that people believed in him and his vision. They knew he would die before relinquishing his word—and because of that, they stopped fighting. His commitment went beyond force; it touched the conscience of an entire nation.

This is what true authentic leadership looks like. Complete integrity gives you a kind of influence that no amount of force

3 "**Mahatma Gandhi.**" *Biography.com.* Accessed March 17, 2025. https://www.biography.com/political-figures/mahatma-gandhi.

or power can rival. It inspires others to follow not because they fear consequences, but because they trust and respect you. When people know you will stand by your word, no matter what, they respond differently. You lead not just through position, but through presence.

DISCOVERING WHERE INTEGRITY IS LACKING

Integrity isn't about being perfect—it's about being responsible. And that means being willing to see where your integrity is out. Not in a way that's harsh or critical, but honest. Curious. Aware.

Most people look for where they're doing okay. But real leaders ask a better question: 'What am I not seeing?'

If you're only looking at where your integrity is in, you'll miss things. But ask, 'Where is my integrity out? What have I been avoiding, ignoring, or letting slide?' and you'll start to see the places that need your attention.

This is where your power begins to come back.

Look for anything that's incomplete: promises you haven't kept, conversations you've been putting off, corners you've cut, things you've been tolerating. These may seem small—but left unaddressed, they quietly chip away at your confidence, clarity, and leadership.

For example, maybe you see an employee rushing through a project, not doing it as well as it could be done. And you let it slide, telling yourself it's 'good enough' even though you know it's not. These small moments create cracks. And if you keep ignoring them, those cracks spread. Eventually, they show up in your results and in your energy.

That's why, when I feel off-track, one of the first things I do is a full integrity review. I sit down with a blank sheet of paper and make a list of everything that feels unresolved such as things I said I'd do and haven't, people I need to clean up with, areas I've neglected. I write until there's nothing left to write.

Then I make a plan. What conversations do I need to have? What actions do I need to take? What have I been avoiding that now needs dealing with? And I start—straight away. Even before the list is complete, I begin to feel clearer, more grounded, more myself.

Some things can't be resolved overnight. But even then, I communicate. I let the other person know I'm taking responsibility and tell them when I will deal with it. That alone starts to restore integrity.

Sometimes, restoring integrity means making amends. Sometimes, it means following through. Either way, when you take responsibility and bring things back into alignment, something always shifts. You feel lighter—more focused, more at peace.

Integrity brings you back to wholeness.

At the end of this chapter, I'll walk you through **The Integrity Reset Method.** This powerful process helps you see where integrity is out and how to start bringing it back into your life and leadership.

RESTORING INTEGRITY

As a transformational program leader for over 22 years, most of my preparation before an event wasn't reviewing notes or rehearsing content—it was cleaning up my integrity. Many a night before a course was spent emailing people, leaving voicemails for people, cleaning up with people where I'd allowed my integrity to go out. I would walk up to lead the program the next day with very little sleep sometimes, but with full power, and the experience of being whole, clear, and complete, ready to lead a three-day program, bereft of tiredness.

I share this to highlight two things:

First, integrity is not morality. It's not about being good or bad. It's about what works. It's about power, freedom, and workability.

Second, to emphasise that, for all of us, integrity is always going out. If you think your integrity is 100% whole and complete for more than a day, you're in big trouble! That's why the question isn't 'Is my integrity in?' It is rather, 'Where is my integrity out?' Part of you won't want to ask that question. You'll avoid it. You'll justify, minimise, or pretend things are fine. But when you pierce through that resistance and take an honest look, you get your power back. And when you restore integrity, you realise how much the lack of it was weighing you down.

I had to learn this the hard way. When I was being considered for a senior leadership role in my previous organisation, they wouldn't even interview me until I'd completed a full integrity inventory of my entire life. Prior to opening this file, I believed that I had integrity. I'd been leading programs for years. I really believed that I was someone who functioned with integrity. This file asked me lots of questions about my life. And after going through it and answering the questions honestly, I had 64 pages of items to get complete— things I'd forgotten, avoided, or never addressed.

Some were big. Some were small. But they all mattered.

I paid money back to the Royal Air Force. I repaid over-claims to insurance companies. I found ex-girlfriends and apologised for things I had said or done. And with every one of those conversations, something opened up.

I'll share one small example. When I was eight, my friend and I walked into a village shop. While I stood between him and the shopkeeper, he stuffed a whole box of football cards down his shorts. Later, we split the cards between us. That was that.

Decades later, during the inventory, I remembered. I called the shop and asked how much a packet of cards cost and how many were in a box. It came to £11. I told the man on the phone, 'I want to send you a check. My friend stole those cards when we were eight, and I want to pay for them.' He said, 'Were you just in the shop a couple of weeks ago?' 'No,' I said. 'This was thirty years ago.' He was flabbergasted. He couldn't understand why I would bother to do that. I told him, 'I want to pay it back. I want to clean up my integrity.' I insisted on sending the check.

Now, the next time I was in my parents' town, instead of walking past the shop, I went in. This was the first time I'd entered the shop since I was eight years old. It was an enchanting experience, like walking back in time. The smell of the shop hadn't changed. I was able to relax and look around the store. I was free. Prior to this, I'd unconsciously avoided going into the shop. I'd always turned my shoulder away from it as I walked past. I had no idea I was still being impacted by something I'd done when I was eight years old—until I cleaned it up. When you clean things up, something shifts. You'll experience that area of your life differently. And you'll experience yourself differently.

ELEVATING YOUR INTEGRITY AS A LEADER

So how do you start elevating your integrity as a way of being—not just a one-off clean-up?

You make it a habit. You commit to seeing what needs to be done and doing it. You honour your word, especially when no one's watching. You don't cut corners. You don't walk past things that aren't working. And when you fall short (because we all do), you own it and restore what's missing.

Real leadership doesn't come from being perfect. It comes from being responsible. The more you practise integrity, the more grounded, trustworthy, and powerful you become. It's not always easy. But when you start living this way, people notice. They trust you. They respect you. And more importantly, *you* trust you.

Every time you choose integrity in those small moments, you build the strength to tackle the bigger ones with confidence and ease. To illustrate how integrity as a leader might look, here is an example of one of my coaching clients:

Case Study: Franco's Path to Integrity and Prosperity

The following is a real life example of one of my clients whose commitment to integrity changed his life and his business.

Franco ran four businesses, including an art dealership featuring his father's artwork. However, all of his ventures were struggling, and he was in poor health, burdened by stress and mismanagement. The first thing we went to work on was his integrity. I had Franco compile a comprehensive list of issues that needed addressing, from neglected financial obligations to broken promises. Tackling these issues head-on, Franco established regular meetings with his managers and started honouring commitments, both big and small. I held him to account with each item on his list until they were all resolved.

One of the most pivotal moments in Franco's journey came from an issue he was neglecting and not dealing with. (This approach lacked integrity. He wasn't addressing what he knew needed to be addressed.) He knew there was a significant number of paintings that were missing from his father's catalogue. They were missing because his father had painted and sold paintings in his 30s and 40s while working abroad and had kept no records of who he'd sold them to. The catalogue kept track of who owned each of his father's paintings and sculptures and where they were located in the world. Franco couldn't see any way of locating these paintings. Fortunately though, he had a coach—me.

A coach can see outside of your paradigm and ask questions you never thought to ask yourself and make suggestions that wouldn't ordinarily occur to you. My suggestion was, 'Why don't you advertise and offer a reward for anyone connecting you with the owner of any previously undocumented paintings by your father?' He took the coaching, offered a reward, and within six weeks had located, acquired, and resold many of the paintings, making a profit of $17 million. Within three months of working together, Franco improved his financial standing, all four of his businesses reported record profits, and he also regained his health and peace of mind.

Now just to be clear, integrity alone doesn't produce results; it's just a necessary condition for optimum performance. So as a leader, if you're interested in high performance, get interested in integrity.

EXERCISE: THE INTEGRITY RESET METHOD

As in Franco's situation, there are likely areas where you are overlooking issues, letting situations go unresolved, or cutting corners, which all impact the integrity of your leadership. If you're serious about leading with power and clarity, you need a regular practice of reviewing and restoring your integrity. That's what The Integrity Reset Method is for; it's a simple but powerful process to get clear, clean, and back in alignment with yourself, your word, and your vision.

Use a blank sheet in your notebook and work through the following five steps. Don't rush. Take the time to reflect honestly and write everything down. This is for *you*.

Step 1: Choose the Areas of Life You Want to Review
Start by identifying the key areas of your life where integrity matters most right now. These could include:

a. Finances
b. Work or business
c. Home and environment
d. Health and fitness
e. Family
f. Relationships
g. Promises to yourself
h. Promises to others

You don't have to take on everything at once—but be honest about the areas where something feels off, messy, or incomplete. These are often the places where your power is leaking.

Write down each area you want to focus on.

Step 2: Identify What's Incomplete, Unspoken, or Out of Alignment

For each area you listed in Step 1, ask yourself:

- Where have I not kept my word—to myself or others?
- What promises, agreements, or commitments have I not fulfilled?
- What have I been avoiding, delaying, or tolerating?
- Is there anything I need to say, clean up, complete, or make right?

Don't filter. Don't justify. Don't soften the truth. Just write.

Whether it's an email you haven't responded to, a conversation you're avoiding, a mess you've walked past, or a payment you've delayed—it matters. Small leaks create big losses over time. This step is about bringing it all into the light.

Keep writing until you can't think of anything else.

Step 3: Make a Plan to Restore Integrity

Now take your list from Step 2 and create an action plan. For each item:

- Decide what specific action you'll take to restore integrity.
- Set a clear date and time by when it will be done.
- If it involves someone else, write down how you'll communicate with them.

- Be real about what it will take—and make it doable.

You might need to have a conversation, complete a task, renegotiate an agreement, return something, apologise, or recommit.

If you can't do it immediately, acknowledge the delay and let anyone affected know when you'll handle it. That's integrity too—not pretending it's done, but being responsible for when it will be.

Commit to taking at least one action within the next 24 hours.

Step 4: Set Up Accountability and Support
Restoring integrity is easier—and more powerful—when you're held to account.

Choose someone you trust: a coach, a mentor, a colleague, or even a friend. Share your plan with them. Be clear about:

- What you've committed to
- When you'll do it
- How you'll report back once it's complete

Ask them to hold you to your word. Not to rescue you or make you feel better but to support your leadership. When you know someone is going to check in with you, you show up differently.

If no one comes to mind, write down a date when you'll check in with *yourself* and put it in your calendar. Leadership starts with being accountable to *you*.

Step 5: Establish Simple Structures to Stay in Integrity
Restoring integrity is powerful. *Sustaining* it is where the real growth happens.

Look at each area you reviewed. For every item or theme that tends to slip, ask:

- What weekly or monthly structure could help keep this clean?
- What system, schedule, or habit would support me here?
- Where do I need to build in reminders, reviews, or check-ins?

Examples:

- A weekly finance review every Friday at 10am
- A monthly conversation with your partner about shared commitments
- A standing calendar block to follow up on open tasks
- A journal check-in at the end of each day: 'Where was I in full integrity? Where was I out?'

Don't overcomplicate it. Keep it simple. Keep it real. But don't leave it to chance.

Once you've created these structures, you're no longer *trying* to operate with integrity—you're *living* it.

To support all of this—as mentioned in Step 4—I strongly recommend having a coach to hold you accountable. Integrity is always going out. A coach can help you manage it until you've built the muscle to be reliably accountable to yourself.

Uncovering where your integrity is out, and restoring it, needs to become a way of life if you're committed to growing into a powerful, authentic leader. If you're interested in performance, get interested in finding everywhere integrity is missing, compromised, or unclear.

And if you find it's out, don't beat yourself up. That's not the game. Finding where your integrity is missing is not a failure; it's an opportunity to elevate your performance. Think of it like being part of a high-performance Formula One team. You wouldn't berate yourself every time the oil needed changing or the tyres needed replacing. You'd service the car, so it can keep running at its peak.

That's how you need to treat your integrity. It's not about being perfect. It's about staying tuned, staying clean, and running at your best.

Integrity isn't about being flawless; it's about honouring your word, living in alignment with your vision, and staying true to your authentic self, in fittra.

REFLECTION QUESTIONS TO UNCOVER WHERE INTEGRITY IS OUT

1. Where am I not fully honouring my word—to myself or others?
2. Where am I not being true to my authentic self, in fittra?
3. Where are my actions or behaviours out of alignment with my vision?

CHAPTER TAKEAWAYS

» Integrity means being true to your word, leading from your authentic self, and aligning your actions with your vision.

» Integrity is all or nothing—it's either complete, or it's not.

» Integrity is always going out, so you need structures to keep it in.

AUTHOR'S NOTE:

Everything in this chapter is drawn from my own real-world experience, from my time as an RAF Officer, to decades coaching and leading transformational programs across the globe. These principles were shaped through thousands of hours working with real people in high-pressure environments, not borrowed from any training company or proprietary source. What you've read reflects what I've found to be most effective, authentic, and lasting in developing powerful leadership.

Chapter 15

PURPOSE AND VISION- DRIVEN BUSINESS GROWTH

'True growth isn't about doing more for the sake of doing more. It's about doing what matters and doing it in alignment with who you truly are as a leader.'

In Chapter 12, you created a compelling vision rooted in your purpose—a bold, authentic picture of what you're here to cause in the world. This chapter is about using that vision as a compass for how you grow your business. When you lead with purpose and vision, your decisions become clearer, your focus sharper, and your impact greater. True business growth happens when everything you do—from the choices you make to the opportunities you pursue—aligns with the deeper why behind your work.

Have you ever found yourself chasing a revenue goal, sure that if you just hit XYZ you would feel better about your business? That's what happens when you aren't leading authentically. You fall into the trap of chasing external results and pushing yourself to work harder, which often leads to burnout.

Authentic leadership doesn't only focus on goals or external results. It's not about marketing strategies, scaling operations, or chasing profits. Authentic leadership means staying true to who you are while allowing that authenticity to guide every decision, every promise, and every action taken—even when it challenges conventional wisdom or short-term gains. True business growth is about aligning every step you take with your purpose and the vision you've created for your business. For example, the choices you make, the products you sell, the services you offer, who you hire, who you choose as your suppliers, how you expand your business, your company policies, etc.

ARE YOUR DECISIONS ALIGNED WITH YOUR PURPOSE AND VISION?

Running a business comes with opportunities and choices— and sometimes it's hard to know where to put your focus or what decisions to make when. But if you know your purpose and vision, and are committed to them, decisions become easier. You don't have to agonise over choices when you know deep down that the choice is aligned with your purpose and vision, which become your true north.

In every opportunity or moment of decision-making, pause and ask yourself:

- Does this move me closer to my vision?
- Does it align with my purpose?
- Will this still make sense six months or a year from now?

Sometimes what looks like an opportunity is actually a distraction. For example, expanding into a new market may seem like a logical next step. But if it doesn't align with your values or vision, it might not be worth the cost. Authentic leaders are willing to walk away from opportunities that don't fit, trusting that better, purpose-aligned opportunities will come.

THE POWER OF SAYING NO

If you've been in business for any length of time, you've probably said yes to something you knew wasn't right. Maybe you undercharged for a project, took on a client who didn't align with your values, or agreed to do something outside your zone of genius out of fear of missing out. It happens. We tell ourselves we need the work, the money, or the relationship— and saying yes feels safer. But real, authentic growth means learning to say no.

Saying no to opportunities that don't serve you keeps you aligned with your purpose and vision. It stops you wasting time, energy, and focus on things that dilute your impact. It also creates space for the right opportunities—the ones that truly fit. When you're clear on what you stand for, you naturally start attracting clients, team members, and collaborators who share that clarity. You'll attract people who resonate with your purpose, people who want to be part of what you're building.

And here's the truth: when something doesn't align, it's not only *okay* to walk away—it's essential. A short-term *no* often creates the space for a long-term *yes* to what truly matters.

Purpose-driven growth isn't about hustling harder or chasing every opportunity. It's about staying the course. It's a marathon, not a sprint. And if you find yourself saying yes out of fear—fear of missing out, of losing money, or of disappointing others—that's a sign to pause, reconnect with your true self, and if you need to, go back to Part 1 of this book, especially Chapter 7 on fear, and realign.

When you know who you are and stand firm in your authentic self, in fittra, you stop chasing. You lead with clarity and conviction, saying yes only to what aligns with your purpose, your vision, and what truly moves your business forward with integrity.

Case Study: Martin's Journey to Sustainable Growth

I have seen firsthand the power that purpose-driven growth, built on integrity, can have on the people I have coached. One of my clients, who I'll call Martin, comes to mind. He ran a very successful diabetic supply operation in North America. After working with me for a couple of months, he had increased his revenue to a million dollars a week. Martin's purpose was to improve the health of others. The vision he had created, based on that purpose, was to support those with diabetes to achieve better health, while also empowering his employees to achieve bonuses so they could provide good homes, education, and healthcare for their own families.

However, we uncovered a critical issue: his main product, insulin, was being sourced from wholesalers and individuals with excess supplies, and it was not FDA (Food and Drug Administration) approved. The insulin sourcing issue was in conflict with his purpose.

Beyond the integrity issue, there was also a significant risk: continuing to trade non-FDA-approved insulin could lead to high fines, loss of reputation, or even possible jail time.

I had Martin confront the impact this lack of integrity was having both on his business and on him personally. After much soul-searching, Martin made the difficult decision to stop trading in non-FDA-approved insulin. He knew this would come at a financial cost, and initially it did. Halting that production lowered the sales volume and took a toll on his revenue. This made it hard for his employees to earn bonuses—and eventually his entire sales staff quit because of his decision.

Despite this setback, I encouraged Martin to stay true to his purpose. He began researching alternative products in the diabetic market that didn't require FDA approval, allowing him to rebuild his business with integrity while remaining true to his vision. This effectively created a new market for Martin. With guidance and support, he began rebuilding from the ground up. Within three months, Martin had six new employees that he'd trained thoroughly, had sufficient revenue to reinvest in new markets, and—most importantly— had found clarity and peace of mind. He no longer had to worry about being found out by the FDA or facing legal repercussions.

Today, Martin's business continues to grow. He's highly motivated, excited about scaling his operation beyond previous levels, and has learned many new ways to expand his business on a foundation of integrity. He's proud of what he's accomplished, not just in terms of revenue but in his personal growth as well. He's stronger, he has more influence in his industry, and his business is aligned with his greater purpose.

AUTHENTIC GROWTH IS SUSTAINABLE GROWTH

When you build your business from a foundation of integrity, purpose, and vision, growth becomes sustainable. You avoid overcommitting. You say no to what doesn't fit. You delegate with confidence, knowing your team is aligned with what's most important.

True growth isn't about doing more for the sake of doing more. It's about doing what matters and doing it in alignment with who you truly are as a leader.

The more authentically you lead, the more powerfully your business will grow in ways that are not only scalable, but deeply meaningful to you.

OPPORTUNITY TO PRACTISE: MAKING DECISIONS ALIGNED WITH YOUR PURPOSE AND VISION

As you go through your day, whenever there's a decision to make, ask yourself:

'Standing in my purpose and vision, what should I do here?'

Make this a habit. At first, you'll need to remind yourself and practise it, but if you keep doing it, pretty soon it will be easier and easier, and eventually will become the way you operate. You'll start making faster, clearer decisions—and they'll feel better too.

If you feel you need any additional support, please head to www.willsteel.com/freetolead.

REFLECTION QUESTIONS:

1. Have I been focusing on growth for growth's sake?
2. Have I been working in alignment with my purpose and inside of fulfilling my vision?
3. Have I said 'yes' to the wrong opportunities? If yes, was there a moment where I lacked the courage to stay true to my purpose?
4. How can I make decisions that align with my purpose and vision from this point forward?

CHAPTER TAKEAWAYS:

» Growing your business with purpose isn't just achieving external results.

» Saying no to the wrong opportunities creates space for the right ones to show up.

» Weigh every business decision against your purpose and vision, and let this be your true north.

Chapter 16

EMBRACING FAILURE

'If you want to achieve more, perform more, or become more successful, you need to get comfortable with embracing failure.'

We've already talked about redefining success. But in leadership, it's not only important to redefine success, but also to redefine failure. Failure is often seen as something negative, even something to avoid at all costs. You might think of failure as embarrassing or disappointing, as a sign of inadequacy.

But that's not what failure is. Failure is inevitable; it's part of life. Your goal should not be to 'never fail' but to be able to learn and grow from moments when things don't go as planned. In fact, if you never fail in your business, or in your life for that matter, chances are you are living in a very small and constrained way. The more that you grow and the more you work towards a greater purpose, the more you will find yourself in the face of 'failures' or 'mistakes'. Each of these is a chance to learn, pivot, and keep moving forward.

Whenever you try something new, step out of your comfort zone, or aim for a big vision, you're likely to experience some failures along the way. Authentic leaders know that failure isn't an end and that it doesn't define them. Instead, they look at it as a natural outcome of taking risks.

Some of the most successful companies have a policy of trying things out and pushing them to fail. This stress testing is designed to have unworkable ideas fail fast, before anyone has invested too much time, energy, and money in them. In this way, authentic leaders can develop strong ideas and move more quickly towards success.

So, if you want to achieve more, perform more, or become more successful, you need to get comfortable with embracing failure.

FAILURE AS FEEDBACK

Think of a time in your life when you received constructive criticism or feedback that led you to make a positive change. This might have come from a teacher or an employer. When you are open and accepting, feedback can be the spark that ignites real growth.

You can think of failure in the same light. Failure isn't a final verdict on your abilities or your worth. It's simply feedback. Failure occurs when you don't meet your expected outcome, and it provides you with valuable information about what did and didn't work. It exposes blind spots and challenges you, forcing you to reassess. If you look at failure without shame or self-criticism, you can gain insight into how to solve problems, come up with new ways to reach the outcome you're aiming for, and improve your performance.

You can turn failure into a learning tool and use it to your advantage.

GROWTH FROM FAILURE

My earliest example of embracing failure was when I failed my Mathematics GCSE at 15 years old. I didn't sit in the shame that I had "failed". Instead, I chose to retake the course at night school during my first year working as an engineering apprentice. I thought about *why* I had failed and what I could do differently.

I realised that I had not learned the basic steps in calculus while at school, so I decided to make sure I understood every step, starting with the basics. I worked until I fully understood a concept. I didn't jump ahead to the next step. I retook the exam and got an A. My approach didn't just allow me to pass that exam, it also changed the way I viewed mathematics. For the first time, I realised it wasn't difficult— it was one logical step after another. Later in my honours degree in Electronic Engineering at Liverpool University, I specialised in mathematics in my final year. I had gone from failing at the most basic level to succeeding at a very high level of academics.

Another notable failure occurred during my flight training when I failed my instrument rating in the Jet Provost Mk3. This failure was a wake-up call, showing me the gaps in my skills and knowledge. I was suspended from training, and I felt quite lost and dejected. For two weeks, I hung around the station, not sure what was next. But just before my final exit interview, I called the oldest RAF pilot I knew for advice. Tony Madden had been the Admin Officer on my University

Air Squadron. Tony was quite a character. He had lied about his age during the Second World War and flew as captain of Wellington Bombers at 17 years old. He had grit and wasn't the type to take 'no' for an answer.

When I asked him what I should do, he barked, 'You're not fighting for it. Go in there with the Station Commander and fight for it. Bang your fist on his desk and tell him, you're a fu%#ing pilot, and you want another shot at it. Tell him flying is in your blood and you can do this, and that you'll show him if he gives you the chance to prove it. Don't leave his office until he gives you another go!'

So, I took his advice to heart. I walked into the Station Commander's office determined to take a stand for myself. He reviewed my file and said I had good marks in all areas— and that it was disappointing I had failed. I spoke up, saying, 'I am a good pilot. Flying is in my blood. This was just a glitch. I'll show you if you give me another shot.' I stood firm and went for it, spending two hours pleading my case (a far cry from the cursory 15-minute exit interview he had expected). I was going to get him to give me another chance or get myself thrown out of his office.

Eventually he said, 'Okay, well, it's obvious that you haven't given up, so I'm going to give you another shot. I'll speak to the Chief Flying Instructor, and we'll work out what we are going to do with you.' I could not believe it. Tony's advice worked, I was still a pilot. I still had a chance.

What happened next was: I was given one trip to go and do whatever I wanted. I did some aerobatics and low-level navigation, which I was good at. I then had two trips of instrument revision where I saw what I had missed during my training. I was given the test again. And this time I aced it. I had learned from my failure to keep fighting and never give up, no matter how bad things looked.

If you keep going, you can succeed. If you give up, you definitely lose.

It's natural for us to feel disappointed or frustrated when we fail. But if we look at failure not as a moment that defines us but as an opportunity in growth, we build resilience. We learn how to bounce back from setbacks and to keep pushing forward even when things get tough.

CREATING A TEAM MINDSET AROUND FAILURE

In leadership, embracing failure without making people wrong for it can help you create a culture where your team feels safe to take risks and innovate. This doesn't mean that you have to tolerate somebody repeatedly failing in their job. What it means is that when people do fail, you look together to see why they failed and determine what can be done about it. Functioning this way will help you grow and develop your people in the long-term.

Recently, I saw this in action with the sales team as they were filling a program that I was due to lead in Casablanca, Morocco (the same one I mentioned in Chapter 12). Things weren't going well. It was only two and a half weeks before the course, and they had only registered five people in the program. I decided to step in and meet with the whole team every morning leading up to the course starting. But I didn't come in ready to scold them or tell them what they were doing was wrong. Instead, the first thing I did was listen to them. The team talked about the difficulties they were having, mostly that the people they were calling couldn't afford it. And, as a team, they were struggling to make sales.

I told them we were not in the sales business—we were in the business of transforming people's lives —and to stop referring to the people registering as a sale, to not even call themselves a sales team. They were renamed the Registration Team. Their job was to speak to people and get into their world, find out what they were dealing with, and what they wanted to change in their lives, *then* talk about how participating in the course could really help them with that. Their job was to empower people to take their lives on and commit to their own transformation.

In the next two weeks the team fell in love with the people they were speaking to and experienced the joy of supporting them to take this first step. Every morning each team member shared their successes, what worked, and also where they fell short. I was able to coach them in becoming masterful at supporting people to take the leap. By the day of the program, 120 people registered—and the newly born Registration Team grew, developed, and succeeded.

TURNING FAILURE INTO YOUR NEXT SUCCESS

One of the most powerful aspects of failure is its potential to be the catalyst for your next big success. If you don't give up or beat yourself up, but instead look for what was missing that caused you to fail, and go to work on that to correct yourself, failure can be seen as a valuable part of the journey. When I was given another chance at the instrument rating test after failing, I was determined to succeed. I took the opportunity to learn from my mistakes and correct what I'd been doing wrong. Instead of chasing the dials, I focused on flying the aeroplane, and this ultimately led me to passing the test and becoming a better pilot.

The key to turning failure into success is persistence. You only truly fail when you quit. If you keep going, learning from what did not work and adapting, success becomes inevitable. Failure is not the end—it's an opportunity to recalibrate, fine-tune, seek input, and learn from your mistakes, such that you can improve and accomplish your long-term goals.

REFLECTION QUESTIONS

Think of a moment from your past where you failed. Ask yourself:

1. What did I learn from that failure?
2. How have I implemented what I learned?
3. What would I say to my younger self, knowing what I know now?

CHAPTER TAKEAWAYS

> » Failure is an inevitable part of life and leadership, especially when you're working towards something big or stepping outside of your comfort zone.
>
> » Failure isn't a final evaluation—it's feedback you can learn from.
>
> » If you commit to view failure positively, it can become a powerful driver for growth and self-improvement.

Chapter 17

THE IMPORTANCE OF A STRONG SUPPORT NETWORK

'It's easier to achieve your goals and realise your vision when your environment is optimised with a powerful network of supporters.'

Think back to who you were when you started reading this book. What have you learned about yourself? What limiting beliefs have you uncovered? Do you now have a vision that lights you up and inspires you? And how have you grown, as a leader and a person?

Now, you have the lessons in place. You have the knowledge. It's time to move forward in your journey. This will be difficult if you try to do it alone.

Authentic leaders don't just know how to empower others—they are aware of what they need to be empowered themselves. They understand the value of optimising their environment to support and encourage them as they move forward.

THE POWER OF HAVING A COACH

One of the most effective ways to stay connected to your vision and ensure you are leading from your authentic self is by working with a coach. A coach is invaluable in not just giving you information and advice, but also in helping you see the blind spots and limiting beliefs that are hindering your growth and effectiveness. Often, we don't realise the unconscious barriers we create for ourselves—whether it's fear of failure, self-doubt, or old narratives that no longer serve us. A coach who understands this work can help you put the lessons you've learned in this book to greater use. They can also help you uncover more limiting beliefs that you have yet to discover. Without a coach, you may eventually get to where you're going. But with a coach, you'll get there much faster.

Just as an Olympic athlete or a world-class boxer hires the best coach they can afford to reach their peak performance, the same applies to leadership. If you are serious about becoming the best leader you can be, and want to achieve your goals more efficaciously, hire the best coach you can afford. When you invest in a coach, you're investing in yourself and your business. According to research, the return on investment for business owners who hire a coach is a median of 788 percent.[4]

To sum up the idea,

'The best investment by far is anything that develops yourself, and it's not taxed at all.'

—Warren Buffett, 2022 Berkshire Hathaway annual shareholder's meeting

4 Laker, B. (2023, July 21). *Every Leader Can Benefit from Coaching. Here's Why.* Forbes. https://www.forbes.com/sites/benjaminlaker/2022/10/04/every-leader-can-benefit-from-coaching-heres-why/

MASTERMINDS

Alongside coaching, consider joining a Mastermind group. Masterminds bring together like-minded individuals committed to similar goals. These groups provide a space for shared learning and new perspectives. The relationships you build in Mastermind can become an integral part of your support network, strengthening and optimising your environment.

BUILDING A POWERFUL SUPPORT NETWORK

The most important person you can bring into your support network is a coach or a mentor. But there are other key players you need for a strong support system, including peers, trusted advisors, and even employees who share your values and commitments.

When you think about your support network, consider people from different areas of your life—people who challenge you, hold you accountable, and provide insights that expand your thinking. Your network should provide an outside perspective, a sounding board, and people with whom you can celebrate your wins and accomplishments.

Rather than being on your own, it's easier to achieve your goals and realise your vision when your environment is optimised with a powerful network of supporters. It's also essential for you to find ways to contribute to those in your network. Doing so will in fact empower you: The more you give, the more you get.

Case Study: Shawn's Journey to Freedom and Success
Shawn owned a chain of four auto body shops. During the

economic downturn caused by the pandemic, his businesses struggled and he found himself working excessively long hours, trying to keep his business afloat. The long hours were killing him. He came to me desperate to find a way to have his business survive, saying, 'If we can just pull in around $2.5 million, we should be able to keep the lights on.'

When I asked him what his vision was for his business, he couldn't see anything further than just surviving. I worked with him to create a vision where his business not only survived but he was living the life of his dreams, his business virtually ran itself, and he had lots of time to spend with his family.

It was clear that Shawn needed to learn how to delegate effectively. The first thing I had him do was to hire four managers—one to oversee each shop, freeing up his time to focus on strategic planning, cost effectiveness of operations, and business development. This transition wasn't easy, as Shawn had always been deeply involved in every aspect of the business. However, by empowering his managers and trusting them with more responsibility, he discovered that his team could handle much more than he had given them credit for.

A significant breakthrough came when Shawn had to deal with an overpaid and underperforming employee who happened to be his brother. The emotional complexity of the situation had paralysed him. Through coaching, Shawn navigated this sensitive issue by separating his personal feelings from the professional necessity of the conversation he needed to have. I said, 'Look, tell your brother that you and he have two relationships, one as brothers who love each other profoundly, and nothing is ever going to get in the way of that. And the other relationship is one of boss and employee. You need to have a conversation with him as his boss and ask him if he's okay with that.'

When Shawn addressed his brother this way, his brother agreed—for he too had been troubled by what was going on in the business. This clarity of context for the communication that needed to happen allowed Shawn to handle the conversation with compassion and firmness, leading to a positive resolution while maintaining their close relationship as brothers. They worked it out together.

By delegating effectively, creating a clear vision, and addressing difficult situations head-on, Shawn's business not only survived but grew exponentially. Instead of scraping to make $2.5 million to keep the lights on, they made $7 million in the year I worked with him. In addition, he reduced his workload dramatically, working only 12 hours a week instead of 60 to 70 hours. He recently received a substantial offer to sell his business for 23 million dollars. Shawn transformed his business and his life. He not only reclaimed his time, but he also built a highly efficient business with self-driven employees who took ownership of the organisation's success.

THE PATH FORWARD

Shawn needed coaching. He couldn't see what was right in front of him. He couldn't bring himself to confront the challenges he faced. And he couldn't visualise where he was trying to go or what he was trying to accomplish. This is the case for so many leaders and business owners. Often, you're so close to the business that you can't see things objectively.

As you move forward, remember that the biggest investment you can make in your business is investing in yourself. When you hire a coach, that's exactly what you're doing. You're saying, 'I know I have the ability, but I'm not seeing what I need to see right now to get my business and myself where I want to go. I need help, and I need to increase my speed.'

Ultimately, remember this: Optimising your environment with a strong support network will help you reach your goals faster and more efficiently than trying to go it alone.

CONCLUSION

Take a moment to reflect on the transformative journey we've been on and everything you've uncovered.

In Part 1, we focused on identifying and freeing ourselves from the limiting beliefs and unconscious patterns that hold us back. We explored:

- How our interpretations and the decisions we made in early moments of life formed limiting beliefs that changed the way we showed up in the world (and how those beliefs get reinforced over time).
- The power of uncovering those moments and rewriting the narrative we formed at the time.
- How to discover our true, authentic selves—the part of us that is whole, unlimited, and free.
- How to break away from fears, negative emotions, and the automatic reactions and patterns we repeat over time.
- How to stop striving for results to try to fix yourself and chase an external definition of success.
- And how to stop self-sabotage.

Then in Part 2, we explored how to tap into our authentic leadership. We covered:

- Redefining 'leadership' and learning to lead from our true selves rather than how we think we're supposed to be.

- How to discover our purpose and create a vision that inspires both ourselves and those we lead.
- How to empower, influence, and motivate others.
- The value of integrity.
- The importance of growing a business with purpose and vision instead of focusing on external results or short-term wins.
- How to view failure in a different light, using it as a learning tool instead of a final evaluation.
- And the importance of optimising our environment with a strong support network.

This book is about much more than strategies or business tactics—it's a guide to discovering and embracing the powerful leader that lies within you. This means shedding everything that doesn't belong: the narratives, the decisions, the limiting beliefs, and the external ideas, and embracing who you truly are. At the core of your being lies your true, authentic self—the essence of who you are, in fittra. It's where you are both the drop in the ocean and the ocean itself. You are everything and nothing. Here, you experience a profound connectedness with both your true self and those around you. It is this *you* that has the power to make the biggest difference in the world.

Unleashing your hidden leadership genius doesn't require adding anything—it's about freeing what's already there.

I hope that you can now move forward knowing that you are not limited like a trained flea. Anything you truly desire that's in alignment with your authentic self is possible for you. You, in your most authentic state, are limitless—so whenever you start believing thoughts that you are not, you are moving away from your true essence.

This journey of being Free to Lead is ongoing. It requires continuous self-awareness and work. But with the tools, insights, and practices outlined in this book, you now have a framework to recognise these moments and transform them into opportunities for growth. You have the power to lead authentically and with integrity. The more you do this, the more you will inspire and influence those you lead.

And remember to stay connected to your vision. Keep verbalising your vision and sharing it with those around you. This will not only empower you, but it will inspire, influence, and empower the people you lead.

If you find yourself wanting additional support, my team and I are here to help you continue your journey of authentic leadership. Whether it's through coaching, guidance, or personalised strategies, we'd be honoured to support you as you step fully into the leader you are meant to be. Feel free to reach out to us at www.willsteel.com/freetolead., or email us directly at info@willsteel.com.

Also, as a reminder, if you haven't already, I encourage you to download the free video where I work with clients to uncover and dismantle their limiting beliefs. And if you have, consider watching it again—you may be surprised at the fresh insights you take away. You'll find it at www.willsteel.com/freetolead.

With love and best wishes for your continued success,

—Will

About the Author

William Steel is an internationally respected transformational coach and leadership expert who has spent over two decades empowering leaders to uncover their true potential and lead with clarity, purpose, and authenticity.

A former Royal Air Force pilot who graduated with the prestigious Leadership Trophy from The Royal Air Force College Cranwell, Will's early career took him from global military operations to the commercial cockpit. Yet it was a deeper calling—to help people transform their lives—that inspired his next chapter. For over 21 years, he served as a senior leader with one of the world's foremost organizations in personal and professional development. In that role, he not only delivered transformational programs to over 90,000 individuals across 26 countries and 18 languages but also trained, mentored, and developed fellow leaders to deliver these programs and create lasting impact.

Will's coaching spans CEOs, entrepreneurs, scientists, creatives, and changemakers. With an ontological approach that reveals hidden beliefs and blind spots, he helps clients dismantle the constraints that limit their performance and fulfillment. His work enables people to act freely, lead powerfully, and create results that once seemed impossible.

Today, Will travels extensively, particularly across the Middle East, where he leads programs and coaches world leaders to fulfill their visions. When he's not working, you'll often find him surfing warm waves in Costa Rica or spending time with his two grown-up sons, Daniel and Jamie, who live in Bologna, Italy. His constant companion is Bubbles, his little maltipoo, who is never far from his side.